Launching the Entrepreneur Ship

Why Entrepreneurship Is Alive and Well and

How You Can Start Your Own Business Today

Allon Lefever

with Mike Yorkey

WordServe Literary
7061 S. University Blvd., Suite 307
Centennial, CO 80122

Cover Design ©2017 WordServe Literary
Book Layout ©2013 BookDesignTemplates.com / Keely Boeving

Launching the Entrepreneur Ship / Allon Lefever. -- 1st ed.
ISBN (Softcover) 978-1-941555-33-0
ISBN (Hardcover) 978-1-941555-34-7
This book was printed in the United States of America.

For bulk purchases of *Launching the Entrepreneur Ship,* please contact Allon Lefever at (540) 421-6888 or by email at allon.lefever@emu.edu.

For information on Allon Lefever and *Launching the Entrepreneur Ship*, please visit his website at www.LaunchingtheEntrepreneurShip.com.

ENDORSEMENTS

"Filled with engaging real-life stories, astute observations on what it takes to launch a business, and just the right amount of encouragement, *Launching the Entrepreneur Ship* sails right along. Let Allon Lefever captain your entrepreneurial effort."
—Rick Warren, author of *The Purpose-Driven Life* and pastor of Saddleback Church

"In *Launching the Entrepreneur Ship*, Allon Lefever shares his entrepreneurial experience, which will give you good, solid advice as you contemplate moving forward with your own ideas. As he states in his book, 'There is always room for entrepreneurs in this crazy world in which we live.'

"His advice comes with authority and clarity that any budding entrepreneur desperately looks for. If you have a desire to be an entrepreneur, this book will help you find your way through passion and perseverance."
—Annie Beiler, founder of Auntie Anne's Pretzels

"Allon Lefever is a rare breed. He is an academic with a library to show for it, an entrepreneur with a string of successful business ventures, a philanthropist who has shared his money and experience with numerous worthy organizations, a respected professor, and now a published author. He draws from all these disciplines to write a readable and practical book. Anyone interested and gifted in the field of entrepreneurship will do well to read *Launching the Entrepreneur Ship*. It covers all the bases."
—Edgar Stoesz, author of *Doing Good Better* and former chairman of the board for Habitat for Humanity

"The valuable business and life lessons expressed in these pages need to be shared. For those of us who have been on the receiving end of Allon Lefever's wisdom and leadership, we are certain that many will benefit from *Launching the Entrepreneur Ship*."

—Marlene Wall, president of LCC International University in Klaipėda, Lithuania

"Where most people only see change, the entrepreneur sees opportunity. Most of us lived wide-eyed through the technological revolutions of the 1980s and 1990s—the invention of the PC, the Internet, and the World Wide Web. Allon Lefever and his son Rod saw opportunity. They started an ISP in 1993 and reaped the benefits. Allon distilled his hard-earned business lessons for a generation of college students, and now he's summarized those lessons in the highly readable *Launching the Entrepreneur Ship*, so you, too, can launch your ship!"

—Ken Yoder Reed, novelist and recruiting businessman

"Like a seasoned ship captain, Allon Lefever knows both the thrill of the launch and the ride over the rough seas of entrepreneurship. He gives great advice to young and old, to those just thinking about a new business and those who have started many. The book reads fast, but its wisdom will last."

—Shirley Showalter, former president of Goshen College

"If you're looking for a practical and motivating guide to entrepreneurship, Allon Lefever's book is for you. Packed with captivating personal examples, values, and advice from his lifetime of practicing and teaching entrepreneurship, this highly readable book delivers what it promises."

—James M. Harder, Ph.D., president of Bluffton University in Bluffton, Ohio

"You wouldn't launch a voyage without a nautical chart—and don't launch a business without *Launching the Entrepreneur Ship* on deck. Engaging, entertaining, and, most importantly, educational, this book will guide you past the shoals to success. You couldn't find a better captain than Allon Lefever."

—David Snell, president and co-founder of
The Fuller Center for Housing

"All those ready to take the leap into a new business should check in with Allon Lefever and his new book *Launching the Entrepreneur Ship*. He is encouraging but realistic as to what it takes to overcome start-up headwinds, gain strategic speed, and ultimately build a successful enterprise. These pages are filled with 'been there, done that' wisdom gleaned from decades in the business trenches."

—Robert L. Briggs, American Bible Society senior vice president

"*Launching the Entrepreneur Ship* is a playbook that every entrepreneur needs to have. If you're wondering if you have what it takes to become an entrepreneur, you'll know what to do after you finish Allon Lefever's excellent book."

—Cary Summers, president of the Museum of the Bible
in Washington, D.C.

"An entrepreneur with heart, Allon Lefever shares his fascinating entrepreneurial journey with a delightful blend of historical context, personal experience, and sage business advice. Read *Launching the Entrepreneur Ship* and set sail on your own adventure."

—Carol W. Hamilton, former director of the Center for Entrepreneurship at James Madison University

"The Bible's first page shows God at work—creating and innovating—just like today's entrepreneurs, who still build enterprises to help sustain creation. Open Allon Lefever's toolkit, and you'll find not only traditional topics like capital, risk, and business plans but also values, ethics, and other spiritual metrics of the divine image. His sprightly style is a delight to read with its blend of exuberance, reality checks, and riveting illustrations from his rich career. Every entrepreneur, whether start-up or seasoned, will benefit from this book."

—Wally Kroeker, former editor of *The Marketplace* magazine, a MEDA (Mennonite Economic Development Associates) publication

"I especially liked the way Allon Lefever placed great significance on the importance of every entrepreneur preparing a Values Statement, which is instrumental in developing your business culture."

—Michael A. Stoltzfus, president and CEO of Dynamic Aviation

"Allon Lefever delivers with precision the laser-like essentials of entrepreneurship, concentrating on right-side-up leadership, deep curiosity, and a passion for excellence. *Launching the Entrepreneur Ship* exudes conversational warmth, like heart-to-heart advice over coffee. Allon's narrative is seasoned with the breadth of wisdom that only comes from long immersion in business, education and philanthropy.

Yes, he knows whereof he speaks. Not only did Allon personally share his insights with our start-up tech company, but he also helped us pilot our 'entrepreneur ship' through a rewarding exit, with skill and enthusiasm. Then, Allon modeled values-centered leadership—paying it forward and encouraging us to reinvest our time, talent, and treasure. Not just in our start-ups, but outwardly, for the global village."

—Sid Burkey, president of Burkey Farms in Milford, Nebraska

"When an author has sat on more than sixty boards of directors, it's worth sitting to read his reflections. It's refreshing whenever business theory is painted on a rich canvas of experience."
—Jerry Pattengale, Ph.D., author and University Professor at Indiana Wesleyan University

To Doris, for being there every step of the way with me...

To my entrepreneurial children: Rodney, Jeffrey, and Debra, and their spouses: Lauri, Michelle, and Ross

To our wonderful (and delightful) ten grandchildren: Brooke, Max, Allon James, Ben, Kate, Ellie, Emmy, Maris, Orin, and Lenci

CONTENTS

A Note to the Reader

BY ALLON LEFEVER

S o, do you have an idea?

A really good idea?

How would you like to transform your idea into a successful business?

How would you like to get innovative ideas on how to operate that business?

And if so, would you like to understand how to become a values-centered entrepreneur?

I've written *Launching the Entrepreneur Ship* from a deep sense of understanding about the importance of entrepreneurship in America and around the world. It's my firm belief that there's never been a better time to become an entrepreneur, and that's because of the Internet, which opens up tremendous opportunities for those willing to act on their dreams—opportunities that weren't available just a few years ago or even a few months ago.

I'm aware that books on entrepreneurship often read like boring manuals with fifteen steps to do this or do that when starting a business. Other entrepreneurship books are more like an autobiography of the entrepreneur, such as *Display of Power* by Daymond John of *Shark Tank* fame or *Pour Your Heart Into It* by Howard Shultz, the CEO of Starbucks.

My easy-to-read book is a unique hybrid. While *Launching the Entrepreneur Ship* is focused on how to become an entrepreneur, I also integrate my journey as a successful entrepreneur to help you understand what it takes to start up your own business.

In the following pages, I describe how to go about taking your product or service idea and turning it into a flourishing company by sharing more than eighty real-world examples as well as engaging stories from my thirty-five years in the business world. These illustrations, as well as the lessons I've learned, are typical of the many personal decisions that entrepreneurs encounter and offer you a rare glimpse into what it truly takes to become a successful entrepreneur.

Having help start twenty-two businesses, having served in senior management positions in agriculture, manufacturing, and Internet-provider companies, having served on corporate public boards and private boards, as well as many nonprofit boards, and having helped obtain over $4 billion in capital, I believe I bring the right amount of hands-on experience to the table. But there's another aspect that drives me to write *Launching the Entrepreneur Ship*, and it's that I have increasingly come to value the role of family businesses and the importance of entrepreneurs who start from a dream or a need they observe in the marketplace.

While I have nothing against large corporations, and many of them do good things for society, there is a special beauty in the smaller, community-focused family businesses and the successful entrepreneurs who have a personal relationship with their associates. The positive impact these entrepreneurs make to improving their local communities—and their encouragement for their employees to be involved in their neighborhood—is often critical to the well-being and improvement of our nation's cities and towns. On top of that, and close to my heart, is the fact that entrepreneurs have the unique opportunity to form value-driven companies. The importance of values and culture in guiding your business and your personal life cannot be underestimated.

Finally, you will notice that I use the analogy of launching a business to that of launching a boat or ship. My premise is that if you want your ship to "come in someday," then, by golly, you better launch your boat and set sail today to pursue your dreams.

And may all those dreams come true.

ONE

So You're Thinking About Becoming an Entrepreneur . . .

"Build a better mousetrap, and the world will beat a path to your door."
—Ralph Waldo Emerson, 19th century American essayist and poet

"Entrepreneurship is one of the greatest platforms for large-scale social change."
—Allon Lefever, author of *Launching the Entrepreneur Ship*

I remember the Christmas of 1991 well.

Our son Rod was home after finishing his fall semester at Tuck School of Business on the University of Dartmouth campus in Hanover, New Hampshire. Twenty-five years old at the time, Rod was a semester away from finishing a two-year Masters of Business Administration program after earning his undergraduate degree in business at Goshen College in Goshen, Indiana.

Rod, the oldest of three children, had always made my wife, Doris, and me proud. He seemed to have a nose for business ever since he was a young kid growing up in our hometown of Lancaster, Pennsylvania, gateway to Amish Country. When Rod was in junior high, we lived in a place called Strasburg Redwood Lodges, which had twenty-three small cabins scattered across a couple acres of woodland with room for a red barn and a Shetland pony. One summer, Rod decided that he could earn some spending money by hitching our pony to a wagon and offering rides to the city families that rented out cabins for the week. I can still remember the cute sign he fashioned on a piece of cardboard: "Pony Rides for 10 Cents." Rod also planted and harvested pumpkins that he sold at a roadside stand and raised rabbits for sale at a local farmer's market. He was an entrepreneurial kid with a piggy bank that he emptied regularly at our local bank.

When Rod came home for the holidays from his graduate studies in New Hampshire, we sat down for our traditional

Four generations of Lefever entrepreneurs: my grandfather Harry; my father Elvin; myself; and my firstborn Rodney.

Christmas dinner—Doris always served beef fondue with savory sauces—with our two younger children, Jeff and Debbie. As we dipped chunks of meat into a boiling broth, Rod described a "private bulletin board service" that was available in a computer lab that students could use any time.

"What's that?" I asked. I didn't see how computers and bulletin boards mixed.

"It's really great," Rod responded with excitement in his voice. "I was using this computer in the lab, and another guy showed me how I could find research papers at another university through a computer network that connected the two schools. I could even access information at the U.S. Library of Congress using a computer. It was amazing."

"That's interesting," I allowed.

I wasn't much of a tech person. Sure, I had learned to use an IBM "personal" computer to type memos, but I did business the old-fashioned way at High Industries, where I was Senior Vice President of Affiliated Companies in charge of running a half-dozen wholly-owned businesses. Getting my job done meant attending a lot of meetings, taking and making a zillion phone calls, and reading reports until my eyeballs hurt.

"No, Dad, it's more than interesting. This new computer thing is going to revolutionize the way communications are done worldwide. That's what my professors are saying."

Six months later in June 1992, my son received his MBA and entertained a slew of job offers upon graduation. Most were from banks, but the financial institutions that offered the most money would have taken him abroad to places like London, Paris, and Singapore. Instead of moving to a foreign country, Rod chose to stay close to home and become a project analyst with Farmers First Bank in Lititz, Pennsylvania, about ten miles north of Lancaster.

At Farmers First, Rod was given access to the bank's computers, which were starting to electronically "network" with six other branch offices. Because of his familiarity with computers, Rod's superiors asked him to manage their network in addition to his main job, which was in the area of researching and analyzing potential bank acquisitions.

My son had always been interested in computers. He came of age when personal computers or PCs were becoming commonplace at work and in the home. After graduating from Goshen College in 1988, he trained executives on how to use popular software applications—WordPerfect, Lotus, Excel, and DOS—for a High Industries company called The Office Works, Inc. (At the time, I was chairman of the board for The Office Works, which was a forerunner to the Office Depots and Staples of today.) Then during his summer break at Tuck Business School in 1991, he helped revise the second edition of a book named *Fun of Computing* by John Kemeny, a computer scientist at Dartmouth best known for co-developing the BASIC programming language. Now Rod was putting all that computer knowledge to work.

At Farmers First, he read tech magazines like *InfoWorld, Byte,* and *PC Week* to stay abreast of the rapidly changing landscape in computing. One of the magazine's cover stories featured the "World Wide Web" that had been developed at CERN laboratories in Switzerland in the early 1990s. A handful of primitive websites were available, but it wasn't until the release of a "web browser" known as Mosaic in 1993 that anyone could access these websites via a modem connected to phone lines. In those early days, however, it could take twenty minutes for a single page to load, prompting early enthusiasts to call the experience the "world wide wait."

That would change—rapidly.

Hearing About the Internet

Also following the advancements in computers was a good friend of mine, Carlton Miller, who was the chief financial officer at The Office Works. Even though the world of finance was his domain, Carlton was a bona-fide "techie" fascinated by the early bulletin boards and websites that contained what he called "tons of interesting information."

Sometime in early 1994, Carlton also mentioned this thing called "the Internet," which was the same term Rod was talking about. I like learning about new stuff, but my head spun from acronyms I'd never heard before like URL (for Uniform Resource Locators) and GUI (graphical user interfaces). At any rate, I thought Carlton would find a kindred spirit in Rod. "You guys should get together because I don't know what you're talking about," I said to Carlton.

And that's what Rod and Carlton did for the next year as the Internet exploded like a supernova. Rudimentary video games like Space Invaders and Pac-Man were popular online as well as a new phenomenon called "chat rooms," where people could say anything they wanted anonymously (which can be a good thing or a bad thing, of course). To be part of this new technology, you had to be able to connect your home computer to the World Wide Web via an Internet Service Provider, or ISP, using a dial-up connection through telephone lines. No wireless in those days.

In 1993 and 1994, ISPs popped up in major metropolitan markets like New York, Philadelphia, and Washington, D.C., but in the hinterlands—like southeastern Pennsylvania where we lived—accessing the Internet was hit or miss. People could get to the Internet through local bulletin board services, but that was too complicated for neophytes. Most people living outside of major cities couldn't get on the Internet.

Slowly, an idea formed in Rod's mind that he shared with me. "Dad, there's a network out there being developed to dial up and connect to the Internet, but it hasn't reached Lancaster yet. Maybe we should do something about that."

"What do you mean?" I asked.

"I mean starting our own ISP. Perhaps you and Carlton could go in with me. I've been talking to him, and he likes my idea."

By now, I knew that an ISP was an Internet Service Provider. "How much is that going to cost?"

"I've been looking into it. Probably $30,000 will cover the cost of modems, computers, and equipment. The overhead wouldn't be that high. We could split it. I have $10,000 saved up."

Rod was single, and with a good salary at Farmers First, I knew he was salting away a lot of his paycheck. He'd always been a saver.

"What about your job at the bank? You know, people would kill for your position with Farmers First so early in their careers. You want to be sure before you make a move like this."

"Don't worry. I'm not quitting my job right off the bat, not until we see how it goes."

Without much enthusiasm, I told Rod that I'd think about it and get back to him. After he left the house, my good wife, who overheard our conversation but didn't interrupt, said, "Honey, I'm really sort of surprised you didn't encourage Rod more. You're an entrepreneur, so you know what it's like to chase after your dreams. He's not married and doesn't have any financial pressures. It sounds like he might have a good idea."

I considered Doris's words for a moment. This was her sharp intuition on display. "You know, you're probably right," I allowed. Since Lancaster didn't have an ISP, maybe the timing was right to give it a go.

I waited until Rod got to his apartment and gave him a call. (No cell phones in those days!)

"Hey, Rod. Mom and I were talking, and if you think this Internet thing is a home run, then we'll support you. I will help you get started."

"Awesome, Dad! You won't regret it." Rod was excited to hear that I was on board.

A few nights later, Rod and I sat down with Carlton and decided to each pitch in $10,000 to get our ISP going. We wrote a simple business plan and talked about how we could sign up customers.

Rod purchased several routers and made arrangements with the local telephone company to set up our own "point of presence," or PoP, in an extra office belonging to Wentworth Media, which published books and magazines and was based in Lancaster. Wentworth Media gave us the office space because they became an early investor in our ISP, which we called SuperNet Interactive Services. (Within a year, we would buy out their share of the company.) Then Rod hired a couple of tech nerds who had recently graduated from college to keep the modems working. Our son supervised them on evenings after work and on weekends.

In mid-1994, we hooked up our modems to the telephone company and we were in business. Since we were in on the ground floor, we purchased many good domain names. Then the hard part began: finding customers.

We decided to run tiny, two-inch ads in two local newspapers: the morning *Intelligencer Journal* and the afternoon *Lancaster New Era.* "Want to Connect to the Internet?" was the teaser headline. Readers were then directed to come to the Hampton Inn on Tuesday or Thursday night at 7 p.m., where we would give a live demonstration on how you could get on the Internet using our new company.

At first, our newspaper ads drew hobbyists—the type who subscribed to *Popular Mechanics* and attended computer swap meets and trade shows. The first few meetings drew ten or fifteen people to the Hampton Inn, but Rod did a great job beaming a "screenshot" of his computer onto a white screen and showing people all the exciting things you could do on the Internet. What blew people's minds was witnessing how quickly they could get a response from far-away places. Remember, in 1994, fax machines—faster than mailing and more convenient than phoning—were the rage with the public and widely used in office environments. But the Internet's instant communication capabilities were a revelation to those seeing it for the first time.

Usually half of the attendees signed up for service, which was priced at $19.95 a month. For that, they could connect their PCs—Apple computers were barely around—to a 1200 baud modem, which gave them the capability of a dial-up connection with our modems. Presto, they were on the Internet and accessing all sorts of information even though 1200 bauds—a measure of data transmission—was really slow. Then again, 1200 bauds was state of the art in 1994. (Today, the average connection speed is around 30 megabits per second, which is roughly 20,000 times faster.)

Rod started with six modems that he stacked in pyramid fashion with all sorts of cables coming out of the back of each modem since each one needed power and a connection to a phone line. It didn't take too long for that tangle of cables to become a major headache as Rod kept adding modems to the stack whenever we added customers. Business grew rapidly because we were meeting an unmet need in our community and we were committed to superior customer service.

Within six months, we outgrew our back office at Wentworth Media and moved into a basement of a commercial building next door to the phone company. One thing we found was that the best way to have quality phone lines was to be as close as possible to the Bell of Pennsylvania's central office.

We were adding customers by the hundreds each month as people jumped into the Internet with gusto. Within six months, it became apparent that Rod couldn't do it all working nights and on weekends. His tech guys were up to their armpits with keeping the modems going while adding more to the mix. Rod became so convinced that SuperNet was going to be a big success that he offered to quit his well-paying job with Farmers First and become president of our company.

But we really weren't earning any money yet. All the profits were being plowed right back into buying more modems for SuperNet. So Carlton and I made an arrangement with Rod: we would put in additional money to buy more modems, and he would work for almost nothing but receive sweat equity to maintain his one-third share of the company.

"I'll do it," Rod said, who put in notice that he was leaving his safe position at Farmers First Bank for a start-up ISP. I'm sure he received a few odd looks as he cleaned out his desk.

We weren't the only game in town, however. Other mom-and-pop ISPs sprang up like spring tulips in southern Pennsylvania, but we had the inside track and quickly became the preferred provider in the Lancaster market even though the big boys like AOL (America Online), CompuServe, and Netscape had entered the market. For the next couple of years, we rode the Internet wave in a rapidly growing industry.

I'm scrunching some details here, but the next thing we did was to buy smaller ISPs in our market so that we could acquire their customers and make more money . . . which would allow us to purchase more ISPs. Then we formed a partnership with Denver and Ephrata Telephone Co., which provided phone lines and more resources, helping us to become the largest and most-advanced ISP in the South-Central Pennsylvania region. We called ourselves D&E SuperNet, moving from three founders to a logical strategic partnership.

Entering 1997 and 1998, we were competing well against AOL, the 800-pound gorilla, because we maintained a 6:1 customer-per-modem ratio while AOL purportedly had an 18:1 ratio. AOL ticked off a lot of customers when they dialed in and got a busy signal. The ratio was important because there were peak periods when customers wanted to get online at the same time but couldn't since they were all dialing in at the same time.

In February 1998, I got away to our weekend cottage on the Chesapeake Bay to do some thinking. As I looked through a picture window at a tidal basin, I etched out a business plan that would help us become a regional ISP company of significance throughout the Northeast. We would go into smaller markets, acquire the small operators, and plug them into our T3 telephone lines, which had ten times the capacity of a T1 telephone line but only cost about three times more. We would plug these smaller outfits into our superior equipment. Rod had made a good decision early on to use Cisco routers, which were becoming the gold standard.

Once we became big enough, we would seek out a merger with large regional ISPs in other parts of the country and form a national company, which would allow us to "go public" and issue an IPO (initial public offering) on the NASDAQ market. Tapping into fresh investor capital would allow us to have a national profile.

That was the game plan, bold as it was, but we believed the timing was right. This was early 1999, when the "dot-com" boom was still going strong. Stock prices for companies like Cisco and amazon.com were flying through the proverbial roof because anything seemed possible in the brave new world of online commerce. If we could merge with other regional ISPs and form a national presence, we could suddenly become a player in the online world and on Wall Street. This could be our chance to grab the brass ring on the merry-go-round called life.

We found some upfront capital and started researching about 200 Internet providers that operated in suburban and rural markets across the country. Which ones should we ask to become part of our nationwide Internet company? How much stock and cash would we have to offer to bring them into the fold? If we merged with enough companies, how many customers from the farmlands of Pennsylvania to the coast of California would become D&E SuperNet customers?

There was only one way to find out—do our due diligence. At the same time, it was becoming apparent to everyone that D&E SuperNet needed me full time. The problem is that I had a career job with High Industries, which was the largest private bridge builder in the U.S. and owned a large pre-stress manufacturing company that built high-rise garages and owned and managed extensive real estate holdings. As senior vice president, I was responsible for a half-dozen diversified companies. But a chance to be an integral part of a start-up national company—with my son!—in an industry that was literally being invented as I got up each morning was too good to pass up. I could see the massive hours that Rod and Carlton were putting into D&E SuperNet. Could I not give 100 percent as well?

The answer was yes.

While Rod kept the trains running on time and Carlton oversaw the financials, I hit the road and met with dozens of presidents and senior management representing their regional ISPs.

Some of the companies had a large market share in their part of the state. Others were mom-and-pop enterprises with a handful of customers, relatively speaking, gleaned from overlooked pockets of rural America where AOL wasn't available yet.

In the end, we found sixteen firms that would become the fabric we used to sew a patchwork quilt of companies into a nationwide ISP. In early 1999, we invited the principals to attend a "founders conference" in Washington, D.C. where we could get to know each other and lay the groundwork for becoming a national Internet service provider.

A lot of work had to get done as well as precision planning prior to bringing everyone to the nation's capital. Investment bankers expanded our thinking, encouraging us to think nationally instead of only the East Coast. The eighteen-page plan that I had written during my weekend at Chesapeake Bay ballooned to 328 pages when I took the lead in gaining approval from the U.S. Securities and Exchange Commission to issue a public stock offering on NASDAQ. I outlined how we would be folding sixteen regional Internet firms with D&E SuperNet and forming a new company that we would call OneMain.com. In Washington, I explained to the conferees that this would happen all on the same day. Everyone was on board.

You can only imagine how my heart was racing on March 25, 1999, the day of our "poof IPO"—the merging of a bunch of companies that go public simultaneously. We held our collective breath and watched investors swoop in and pick up all 8.5 million shares for sale. Concurrently, on the same day, we formally finalized the acquisitions of the sixteen companies that formed a new company we called OneMain.

What a ride on the NASDAQ stock exchange that first day! Our stock price opened at $29 a share, rallied to $46 a share by 2 o'clock, and closed at $39—a 70 percent gain in one day of trading.

We were the talk of the CNBC finance shows for raising $215 million, making our IPO extremely successful.

Suddenly, OneMain was one of the nation's ten largest Internet providers and doing business in twenty-five states with more than 325,000 customers. I told an *Intelligence Journal* business reporter that we had a plan in place to reach 1 million subscribers in the next year by targeting small towns where residents couldn't get on the Internet through dialing a local number. We called ourselves "Your Hometown Internet."

It wasn't easy producing a 328-page Form S-1 Securities and Exchange Commission document necessary for taking our Internet Service Provider (ISP) company public on NASDAQ in early 1999.

For Rod, Carlton, and myself, our initial $10,000 investment was now worth eighty times that amount in addition to a nice slice of OneMain stock.

Good thing we kept that money in the bank. As everyone knows, the dot-com bubble burst the following year, in 2000, when the NASDAQ peaked but quickly lost 10 percent of its value after Cisco, AOL, and Dell computers were hit with huge sell orders on their stocks. Like a snowball rolling down a hill, the market went south in a hurry. Investor money dried up as hundreds, if not thousands, of dot-com companies reported that they had failed to generate sufficient revenue let alone profits—or even a finished product in some instances. As investors ran for the exits, the rush to cash out became a stampede.

All we could do at OneMain was ride things out after the dot-com crash. For the most part, we were able to hold our own because we were an Internet *provider*, not a dot-com, but we still took a hit in our stock valuation.

In discussing where we stood with Rod and Carlton, the three of us devised an exit strategy: if a nationwide company wanted to swallow us up to gain market share, then we wouldn't stand in the way.

And that's exactly what happened. On June 9, 2000, Earth-Link, the nation's second-largest Internet provider based in Atlanta—AOL was still No. 1—made us an offer that we couldn't refuse. Because EarthLink liked how we had successfully penetrated small-town America, they put a $308 million offer on the table for our 762,000 customers in thirty-five states. (The fact that we didn't reach our one-million-customer goal was another indicator of the soft ISP market.).

After some back-and-forth, we had a deal.

Now, I know that $308 million is a *lot* of money. Lest you think that Rod, Carlton, and myself each took home more than $100 million, then let me dissuade you of that notion. There were seventeen ISPs in OneMain—the Sweet Sixteen plus D&E Super-Net—and each company retained a certain percentage of shares based on their size in OneMain. That said, the three of us did very well when the EarthLink deal closed. From a tiny ISP start-up that operated from the back of a Lancaster publishing company office in 1994, we became multi-millionaires overnight. We were not alone: I estimate that seventy-one individuals became millionaires or multi-millionaires that day.

You could say our ship came in, but more important than the money were the relationships we built throughout the U.S. and the many experiences we treasured. More on that later.

The entire Lefever family celebrated our successful March 25, 1999 IPO (initial public offering) by gathering around the bronze Charging Bull outside the New York Stock Exchange in New York City.

Meanwhile, as part of the merger, EarthLink asked me to stay on as a vice president of acquisitions. Rod was offered a good job in research and development.

EarthLink didn't have a full-time acquisitions guy, so there was a lot of work to do. Suddenly, I was jetting back and forth across the continental U.S., meeting with smaller ISPs interested in being bought out by EarthLink.

I was a road warrior, but even on the infrequent times I got to be home with Doris, I would get a call in the evening from an ISP executive I had been courting in some far-flung western state. A Tuesday night conversation might go like this:

"Allon, good to be in touch with you. Listen, I talked to the board, and we're ready to listen. Can you come out to Fresno and meet with our executive team on Thursday?"

"Sure. I'll be there."

That's the answer that was expected. And then I'd have to tell Doris that we couldn't go to the local theater production we planned on seeing or ask her to cancel a dinner reservation with friends. And then I'd be on a plane the next morning to wine and dine clients that night, which was a crazy and hectic schedule.

If I wasn't in Indianapolis, Indiana, for a meet-and-greet, then I was in Missoula, Montana, sitting at a conference table and outlining the parameters of a takeover deal. There were also at least two trips a month to Pasadena, California, where I interacted with EarthLink's senior management team.

In the back of my mind was a severance package that we had negotiated with EarthLink when OneMain was sold. Anytime during the first six months of the agreement, Rod and I could leave EarthLink and collect a generous payout. Or we could stay and continue with EarthLink, at which time we would be treated like any other employee in senior management, meaning we would receive a far smaller severance package.

Just before the six months were over, Rod and I looked at each other. I know my son, and my son knows me. We had come to the same conclusion: this wasn't working. Too much travel, too many meetings, too many hours. At the time, I was working on thirty-three deals simultaneously around the country.

We left EarthLink at the six-month mark, collected our severance, and thought about what we wanted to do next in life.

Rod decided to go back into banking. As for me, I chose a new career path: education.

At the age of fifty-five, I wanted to teach the next generation how to be entrepreneurs.

A Move to Goshen

When Rod attended Goshen College, a small, private liberal arts college affiliated with the Mennonite Church, I was asked to serve on the board of directors. This was a high honor that I readily accepted. Over the years, professors in the business school invited me to be a guest lecturer. I liked interacting with fresh-faced college students, many of whom were eager to make their mark in the "real world" once they graduated. I felt like I had something to contribute from my diverse real-world experience that would augment the textbook and research knowledge of business school professors. After all, I had been in the business trenches for three decades and sat in the boardrooms of dozens of companies over the years.

In 2001, Goshen was sponsoring a family business program that provided assistance to privately owned businesses, and Goshen's business school was looking for a new director.

I was approached and asked if I wanted the job. Frankly, I was surprised, but I credited Goshen with thinking outside the box.

Goshen's offer came at a time when I had been deliberating about what I wanted to do with the rest of my life. I'd never been the type who wanted to lay on a sandy Caribbean beach and read pulp novels in my "golden" years. I preferred to stay busy and serve others, which is why I sat on various boards as well as participated in mission outreaches for the Mennonite Church, where we had been lifelong members.

The possibility of teaching Goshen's business students was irresistible to me, but Doris needed to be on board. We knew that accepting the new position was a life-changing decision: we'd have to move from our hometown of Lancaster to Goshen— twenty-five miles southeast of Notre Dame University in South

Bend. Goshen was a small city of 30,000 where half the recreational vehicles in the country are manufactured.

Even though the thought of leaving family and longtime friends behind gave us pause, we felt God's leading to go to Goshen. I became director of Goshen's family business program and an associate professor of business. I loved being in the classroom with students eager to learn about the business world.

I thought we would be in Goshen for the long haul, but after two satisfying years, Eastern Mennonite University, located in Harrisonburg, Virginia, called me out of the blue with a proposition: How would I like to become the director of their MBA program?

The opportunity intrigued me because moving to Harrisonburg would put us a three-and-a-half-hour drive away from Lancaster, where Rod, now married, was living with his family. This would allow us to visit our grandchildren more often. Since Harrisonburg was close enough, we said yes to Eastern Mennonite and moved east.

I ended up directing the MBA program for five years and decided to retire. Doris and I returned to Lancaster, but I returned periodically to EMU to teach a course in entrepreneurship whenever time opened up in my schedule.

That said, it's amazing how busy you get when you retire.

These days, I love being an evangelist for entrepreneurship, which is why I'm writing this book. It's my goal to show you what it takes to become an entrepreneur and encourage you to follow your dreams. There's always room for one more good idea in the business world. If you have determination and mettle, you can succeed as an entrepreneur.

So, do you have a killer idea?

Do you want to strike out on your own?

Do you feel stifled in a corporate environment?

Are you ready to work sixty hours a week instead of forty?

If you can answer "yes" to these questions, I can help you. As someone who's helped launch two dozen businesses, consults regularly with budding entrepreneurs, currently serves on eight corporate boards of directors and four nonprofit community boards, I love coaching the next generation of risk-takers and go-getters on what it means to be an entrepreneur and enjoy interacting with college students about entrepreneurship.

I love that word *entrepreneurship*, especially the syllable *ship* because I've met many people who invariably say the same thing: "Someday when my ship comes in, I'm going to start my own business."

"That's wonderful," I say in response. "But if you want your ship to come in, you must first launch a boat of your own. Why would you expect your ship to miraculously show up someday if you never had one in the first place?"

I've seen too many people never get around to launching anything meaningful that has the potential to return with a great reward. They may say that the timing's not right or they don't have enough capital or the barrier to entry to is too high, which are valid reasons to stay on shore. I want to remind you, however, that there's a great body of water out there called the Internet, which is a game-changer for those with the entrepreneurial spirit. The world of e-commerce is rapidly changing the way we do business. All you have to do is ask the CEOs of brick-and-mortar stores about the challenges they face from online shopping.

I firmly believe that this is a great time to think about setting sail and taking your business idea out to sea, where storms are sure to rise but sunny days could be in the forecast. While becoming an entrepreneur is never a pleasure cruise, the chance to control your destiny as you sail for success will drive your entrepreneurial efforts. You can be captain of the ship!

Let me assure you that you will not be alone on the high seas. I'm happy to report that there's been a significant uptick in the number of new entrepreneurs since 2014 following the long financial hangover brought about by the Great Recession. The bursting of the $8 trillion housing bubble in late 2007 led to sharp cutbacks in consumer spending that stifled business investment.

The 2017 Startup Activity Index data from the Kauffman Foundation, a think tank that tracks entrepreneurial trends, shows that the rate of new entrepreneurs have increased more than 15 percent since 2014:

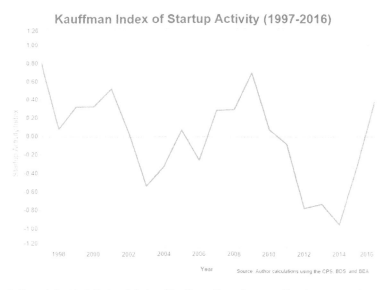

Kauffman Index of Startup Activity (1997-2016)

Perhaps this is why becoming an entrepreneur has become a cool thing to do and even part of today's pop culture. We've all seen reality TV shows like *Shark Tank* and *The Profit*, which feature the pluck and grit of optimistic individuals, couples, and families determined to make their start-up business a success despite daunting odds—or be rudely told that "You're dead to me" by

Kevin O'Leary, aka Mr. Wonderful, on the hit ABC television show seen on Friday nights.

Americans have a long tradition of being dreamers and forward-thinking individuals willing to take big risks—or even risk it all. This nation started on the basis of entrepreneurial freedom and prides itself for its entrepreneurial spirit and independence. Back in 1840, Alexis de Tocqueville, a French diplomat, historian, and author of *Democracy in America*, observed: "What most astonished me in the United States is not so much the marvelous grandeur of some undertakings, but the innumerable multitude of small ones."

More than 175 years later, the Land of Liberty continues to be an innovative, entrepreneurial country. Men and women of every age and ethnic stripe are willing to stake their livelihoods and their futures on a robust business idea occupying their thoughts and burning in their hearts every waking moment of their day. Our entrepreneurial spirit has resulted in small businesses becoming the foundation of our economy, representing 99 percent of all business enterprises and accounting for half of all private-sector employment and nearly two-thirds of new private-sector jobs, according to the Kauffman Index, which catalogs national trends in business startup activity. The Small Business Administration (SBA) estimates there are 28 million small businesses that account for 54 percent of all U.S. sales.

One area of concern that I have is that Millennials—the population cohort between twenty and thirty-five years of age—are starting businesses at a slower rate. It's my observation that Millennials are not making concrete career choices as quickly as their parents did. More are single than in previous generations while others are waiting longer to get married, which can delay getting settled into a career choice. Many are, in fact, freelancing or doing part-time work.

Just as troublesome is the fact that Millennials are coming out of college with more debt than their parents had, which means they are less likely to start a new business since (1) they can't borrow more money and (2) have hefty student loan payments due each month. The rise in student debt coincides with a decline in start-up businesses by Millennials. The number of new entrepreneurs in the twenty- to thirty-four-year-old age group fell from 35 percent in 1996 to 25 percent in 2014, according to the Kauffman Foundation. This decline happened despite the rise in "crowdfunding" sites like Indiegogo.com or Kickstarter.com, where cool entrepreneurial ideas are often rewarded with thousands of $5 and $10 contributions that can jumpstart a business.

I am encouraged by the number of young people jumping into "side businesses" with low-capital expenses, such as making apps for mobile phones or doing website design. Right now, at a hotel I own in Virginia, I have twenty-six employees, mostly young, and eight of them have a cottage business on the side. One has a photography business, another is doing web design, while one fellow started a seasonal landscaping company in addition to working full time for me. Another employee teaches people to paint at local bars holding "paint-and-sip" parties.

Whether you're a Generation Z, a Millennial, a Gen Xer, or a Baby Boomer, this is a great time to board the *USS Entrepreneurship*. Quite frankly, we *need* entrepreneurs because they are the nation's job-creating engine.

One bright spot on the horizon is that 40 percent of fifth- to twelfth-graders said they plan to start a business and/or invent something that will change the world, according to a Gallup Survey taken in 2016. The problem is that less than 5 percent of these students are participating in internships at companies or organizations, prompting Jim Clifton, chairman and CEO at Gallup, to state, "Given the current state of the nation and the outlook for the future, investing in our aspiring young entrepreneurs is essential to developing the next generation of business leaders and community transformers."

I want to be part of the solution when it comes to promoting entrepreneurship. Think about it: when entrepreneurs employ people, those employees re-circulate their wages in the local economy, buying restaurant meals, perusing clothing stores, and shopping at other retail outlets, which keeps those businesses flourishing. Entrepreneurs lift up their communities with charitable contributions, often donating goods, services, and money to worthwhile community organizations and sports teams. A survey of 146 entrepreneurs by Harris Interactive and Ernst & Young revealed that 90 percent of the entrepreneurs surveyed gave money to charitable organizations and 70 percent donated their time.

Entrepreneurs give in other ways that often go unappreciated. When entrepreneurs create new products that benefit society, they improve our lives and raise our standard of living. What would our daily existence be like today if entrepreneurs like Steve Jobs and Bill Gates had not seized their opportunities to build incredible technological empires? Can you imagine life without an iPhone—or any smartphone—or working in a business environment without Microsoft Office at our fingertips?

Harvey Firestone, founder of the Firestone Tire and Rubber Company and one of the first global makers of automobile tires in the early 20th century, once said, "Capital isn't so important in business. Experience isn't so important. You can get both these things. What is important is ideas. If you have an idea, you have the main asset you need, and there isn't any limit to what you can do with your business and your life." Allow me to humbly add that it's equally critical to know how to implement your great idea. That's what *Launching the Entrepreneur Ship* will help you do.

I salute each and every person who decides to leave their job and risk their hard-earned money on starting or opening a new business. There aren't a whole lot of you: according to the Kaufman Index, the Rate of New Entrepreneurs is just 330 out of 100,000 adults, or one-third of 1 percent. While men are more likely to start businesses than women, many women as well as minority ethnic and racial groups, African-Americans, Latinos, and Asians are showing a rising rate of entrepreneurship. The number of white entrepreneurs, however, has been declining for the last two decades.

While it's good news that the number of new entrepreneurs are expanding, I'm also concerned that startup activity is still below the pre-Great Recession peak. On top of that, we are not anywhere near the entrepreneurial levels last seen in the go-go Eighties or the 1990s when the Internet was becoming available in the workplace and people's homes for the first time. The silver lining is that the five-year survival rate of new businesses has increased from 49.8 percent in 2006 to 56.3 percent for businesses started in 2011.

If you're thinking about setting sail, I will show you the steps you need to take before you ever leave the harbor. I will talk about:

• researching your market

• preparing a roadmap for success, starting with a Vision Statement that defines the long-term direction and goal of the company

• preparing a Mission Statement that will define how you fulfill your vision

• preparing a Values Statement that will guide the way you wish to conduct your business (this is one of the most important things an entrepreneur can do, as I'll describe later)

• finding capital and "angel investors"

- developing operating procedures and good planning cycles through strategic planning
- tools to help you make good decisions
- the value of listening to your advisors and/or your board of directors
- moving to the next level as your business grows
- the importance of keeping an eye on the latest technology
- looking to the future—and even having a succession plan in place because we're never guaranteed tomorrow
- giving back—to your employees, to your community, and to those you love

Now that I've turned seventy, I know that I'm entering the twilight of my business career. God has given me incredible blessings as well as wisdom that I want to share with you.

So if you're ready to roll up your sleeves, let's be entrepreneurial together. Let me help you set your entrepreneurial idea on a steady vessel, untangle the ropes holding you back, and give you a gentle push into the great unknown.

Thanks for coming aboard.

TWO

Preparing to Launch

"Without a strategy, the organization is like a ship without a rudder."

—Joel Ross and Michael Kami, authors of *Corporate Management in Crisis: Why the Mighty Fall*

"No entrepreneur ever plans to fail, but many fail to plan."

—Kathleen Allen, author of *Entrepreneurship for Dummies*

"Uncertainty is the enemy of passion."

—Unknown

I'm often asked: What is an entrepreneur?

Many have an image of entrepreneurs as slightly crazy, often eccentric, hair-on-fire individuals who wake up in the middle of the night shouting "Eureka"—a Greek word that means "I've got it!" or "That's it!"

Ancient Greek mathematician and inventor Archimedes was purportedly the first to exclaim "Eureka" thousands of years ago. It seemed that Archimedes was wrestling with the problem of how to determine the purity of gold. One day, while soaking in a public bathhouse, he pondered this great question. When he thought about how the water level had risen when he stepped into the tub, Archimedes realized that the buoyancy of an object placed in water was equal in magnitude to the weight of the water the object displaced.

Have you had a similar "Eureka" moment of self-discovery? Do you have a great idea that could develop into a viable business some day? Could you be an entrepreneur?

I hope you answer yes because there's always room for individuals who see a market for a new business or an opportunity to "make the world a better place" and strike off on their own. But you don't have to leave your present job to do something entrepreneurial. I've met plenty of "intrepreneurs" at businesses and corporations who have affected great change within their companies because of their enterprising ideas. The traits of innovation, creativity, and moving forward with implementing ideas expounded upon in this book are equally essential for nonprofit organizations and are driven by intrepreneurs within those organizations.

No matter where you find them, I admire entrepreneurs and intrepreneurs because they perform like high-wire acrobats without a net underneath them—fearlessly. While the risks and pitfalls are substantial, entrepreneurs can be handsomely rewarded if their business venture succeeds. All it takes is an innovative idea and good execution—which, I admit, are huge tasks—to join the entrepreneur ranks.

The word *entrepreneur* is French, which is meaningful to me because I can trace my forbearers to the Alsace-Lorraine region of France. (I'll share more of that story in Chapter 7.) The etymology of the word, according to dictionary.com, comes from the French word *entrep, which means "to undertake." Thus, the literal translation of entrepreneur is someone who *undertakes* a task or enterprise.

The word *entrepreneur* gained currency during the Industrial Revolution in the late 1700s and early 1800s, a time when new manufacturing processes and technological advances in machinery opened the door to budding entrepreneurs who could build the first steam engine, the first locomotive, the first telegraph, the first telephone, the first light bulb, the first internal combustion engine, the first mass-produced automobile, and the first plane. Nineteenth century economist John Stuart Mill was one of the first to use the term *entrepreneur* in his influential book, *Principles of Political Economy,* to describe those willing to assume both the risk and the management of a new business.

I submit that the times have never been better to become your own boss. Thanks to the Internet and e-commerce, starting your own business costs peanuts in the online world: all you need is a domain name, something to sell or a service to offer, and you're in business.

If only entrepreneurship was that simple. It's not, and I trust you know that. But if you think you have the Next Best Thing, you may be wondering:

Do I have what it takes to become an entrepreneur?

If so, what are the traits of an entrepreneur?

How can I determine if I'm the entrepreneurial type?

I think becoming an entrepreneur starts with being a curious person who views problems as opportunities. You need to be outgoing and self-confident, and you have to multitask and be capable of handling chaos. You have to like a challenge, and you have to be willing to take risks—albeit calculated ones. You have to be willing to work long hours and might have to put in ten-, twelve-hour days because you can't afford to hire anyone to help you. You may have to work a day job to make a living while pursuing your entrepreneurial business evenings and weekends, just like my son Rod did in the early days of SuperNet.

To manage the risks, you must be a thoughtful planner, a quality that I saw in Rod, who was a much better planner than me.

When he introduced the idea of starting our own ISP in Lancaster, I was surprised how thorough his business planning was. He imagined every situation from A to Z and had a response prepared.

So how do you know if you're cut out to be an entrepreneur?

When I was teaching a class on entrepreneurship at Goshen College, the first thing I did was present my students with a ten-question predictor test that would let them know how entrepreneurial-minded they were.

1. Are you a person who can get passionate about something?

2. Do you like to be independent?

3. Do you enjoy problem solving?

4. Can you handle ambiguity?

5. Are you opportunistic?

6. Are you afraid to take risks?

7. Do you see change as challenging?

8. Are you results-oriented?

9. Do you enjoy leading and being in charge?

10. Did you ever have a lemonade stand or a paper route?

Regarding the last predictor, I understand that younger generations may not even know what a "paper route" is, but at one time, young boys (and girls) in the ten-to-fifteen-year-old age range would get up at dawn and ride their bikes through the neighborhood, tossing the local newspaper against the front door of dozens of homes. The discipline of getting up early before school, being responsible for getting the newspaper delivered on time, and collecting the monthly payment taught a trifecta of lessons: be on time, do your job, and make sure you get paid.

A predictor test for the tech world comes from Silicon Valley's Adeo Ressi and Jonathan Greechan of the Founder Institute. These entrepreneurs came up with a short objective test that they use to forecast the likelihood of someone building a successful technology company. They have identified six entrepreneurial profiles:

1. The Hustler
2. The Innovator
3. The Machine
4. The Prodigy
5. The Strategist
6. The Visionary

Without taking the test, where do you think you would place yourself? I know the one that matches the talents God has given me: Visionary. I'd say that Rod is an Innovator—with a bit of Prodigy thrown in—and Carlton is a Strategist. When we got together in 1994, we formed an excellent team.

It's likely, however, you don't have a team yet—it's just you and your dream. That's okay. But if you have a winning idea, have researched an opportunity, and can organize the resources necessary to form an organization that can grow into a viable business, then you can become an entrepreneur.

When Opportunity Knocks

Entrepreneurs come in two main flavors.

The first is what I call an "opportunistic entrepreneur." Launching an ISP company in 1994 before anyone else did in the Lancaster market was a shining example of opportunistic entrepreneurship. But I tip my hat to opportunistic entrepreneurs in New York City who appear out of nowhere with a handful of umbrellas the minute a rain squall soaks Manhattan. Or those guys in Times Square carrying a cooler filled with ice-cold bottles of water on a scorching-hot summer day.

Another real-world example of opportunistic entrepreneurship is the story of Sonia Garcia, who lives in Juarez, Mexico, which borders El Paso, Texas. At one time, Juarez had its own Krispy Kreme doughnut shop, but the franchise store closed when the drug cartels turned Juarez into one of the most dangerous cities in the world.

But what about all those Krispy Kreme fans who were addicted to the gooey glazed confections?

Enter Sonia Garcia, who had an entrepreneurial idea: buy a trunk load of Krispy Kreme doughnuts in El Paso and bring them back to Juarez, where she could sell them for a premium. Call them "black market" Krispy Kremes.

Several times a week, Sonia or one of her sons crosses the border and buys forty boxes of doughnuts from a Krispy Kreme shop at the bulk purchase price of $5 a dozen. Sonia then resells them on busy boulevards in Juarez from the trunk of her car for $8 a dozen, or a 60 percent markup.

You have to admire her entrepreneurial spirit.

The same type of opportunistic attitude happens north of our border on a grander scale. Canadian Michael Hallatt opened a specialty grocery store in Vancouver called Pirate Joe's that sold an eclectic mix of food products purchased off the shelves of . . . Trader Joe's in Bellingham, Washington, sixty miles to the south. Since Trader Joe's didn't operate in Canada, Hallatt saw an opportunity to satisfy Vancouverites' desire for items like Trader Joe's Sea Salt & Turbinado Sugar Dark Chocolate Almonds and Trader Joe's Roasted Garlic & Onion Jam.

Trader Joe's didn't like Pirate Joe's one bit and banned Hallatt from shopping in Bellingham, so the Canadian responded by sending an army of "cats"—paid shoppers—to make the 120-mile

mile round trip and fill up their shopping carts with black bean quinoa chips, gorgonzola cheese crackers, salt-and-pepper pistachios, chocolate-covered edamame, organic tomato basil marinara pasta sauce, pumpkin bar baking mix, organic pinto beans, and mango passion granola cereal, all bearing the Trader Joe's label.

Hallett found out that Canadians were willing to pay a markup of $1.50 or more for their favorite Trader Joe's items, which kept him in business and made him a few loonies—until Trader Joe's sued him for trademark infringement. After a protracted legal battle, Hallatt and Trader Joe's settled out of court, but under the agreement, Pirate Joe's had to close its doors in the summer of 2017.

For every opportunistic entrepreneur like Sonia Garcia and Michael Hallatt, there are what I call "necessity entrepreneurs"—those who fight every day to earn their daily bread. You're apt to find necessity entrepreneurs in Third World countries where there are few jobs and little opportunity to scratch out a living. A necessity entrepreneur might buy a pack of cigarettes and divide it down to a pack of four cigarettes to sell on the streets of Baghdad or hawk packs of Chiclets gum on Avenue Revolución in Tijuana.

Here in this country, a necessity entrepreneur might be a young mom who starts a baking business out of her kitchen to supplement the family income, which isn't enough to support a family of five. In and around Lancaster, Amish women sell handmade quilts, homemade jam, canned fruits and vegetables, beeswax candles, and hand-sewn clothes in tourist shops to supplement their farm income.

Whatever is motivating your desire to go into business, it's important to keep in mind that entrepreneurs come in all sizes, shapes, and income levels but share one common trait: they are passionate about what they do. But passion can take you only so far. From my experience, I believe entrepreneurs need to do four things before they unloosen the tie lines and leave the dock:

• **Get an education.** For every famous college dropout like Steve Jobs, Bill Gates, Mark Zuckerberg, or Walt Disney, there are millions of high school-educated entrepreneurs who didn't make it because they lacked the proper education. It stands to reason that if you're seeking to do something in the area of technology—start a new app, open an e-commerce website, or invent some new electronic gizmo—then you better know a lot about computer programming, the latest software, and the inner workings of a computer.

In addition, being knowledgeable and conversant about a wide variety of subjects—accounting, marketing, economics, management, computer science, writing and composition, and public speaking (since you're likely to be making presentations and sales pitches for the rest of your life)—are the mother's milk of entrepreneurship. It helps tremendously to have a well-rounded education.

Last point: Having a college degree in the field that matches up with your entrepreneurial idea will establish credibility with potential investors and in the marketplace.

• **Seek out lots of experience.** There's no way around it: you better put in the hours and know what you're doing before you launch any enterprise or business. British novelist and theologian C.S. Lewis once said, "Experience: that most brutal of teachers. But you learn, my God do you learn."

Whether you need 10,000 hours to master a skill, which author Malcolm Gladwell posits in his book *Outliers*, or are a quick study, I urge you to buckle down and do the grunt work. I recommend working in the industry nearest to your idea. If you're thinking of starting a delivery service using bikes to move quickly through crowded downtown streets, then visit a large metropolitan city and check out a company that already does those sorts of deliveries so that you can learn more about how that business operates. If you want to start an e-commerce site, then get a job in marketing for a start-up Internet-based company. Get some hands-on experience working in a warehouse or become an account rep who interacts with customers. You can learn so much from customers.

Here's an important illustration of what you need before you become an entrepreneur:

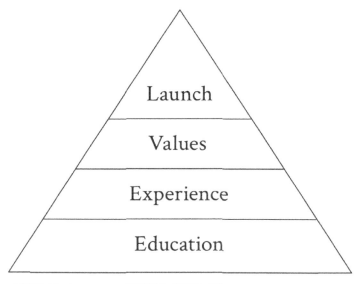

THE ENTREPRENEURSHIP SUCCESS PYRAMID

Research shows that entrepreneurs enhance their chances of success when they have the benefit of experience. Just as you wouldn't want to get into an Indy race car for the first time before the green flag drops at the Indianapolis 500, you want to have lots of practice laps under your belt when you start racing for real. Behind-the-wheel experience counts more than you'd think.

• **Network with others.** Many entrepreneurial experts overlook the value of networking, which is one of the most crucial aspects of being successful in any workplace. Cultivating personal and business relationships both inside and outside of your work often leads to entrepreneurial opportunities. Networking helps you become better connected, grow your business, and give your life greater meaning since you form relationships—sometimes lifelong—with people and colleagues.

There's another aspect about networking that many overlook. Times have changed; we no longer expect to work with the same company for a lifetime—just as corporate executives don't expect you to stick around forever. Making contacts *inside* a company could help you later on if that person gets promoted to the corner office—or moves on to a rival company. The old saying that *who* you know is more important than *what* you know is certainly true when it comes to networking.

• **Have impeccable timing.** It's important to do things in sequence when starting a business. Is this the right time to launch your idea? What's the competition like? Do you have sufficient capital to go into business? What's your "burn rate"—the amount of cash on hand to finance your overhead before you start generating a positive cash flow from operations?

These are important questions that must be addressed before you go any further because timing is everything.

Sometimes in the middle of implementing a plan, one needs to pause when economic data shows a slowdown. Milo Shantz, a friend of mine instrumental in the development of the quaint town of St. Jacobs, Ontario, held up on continuing a huge Farmer's Market addition until the economy improved—even though the sidewalks were already poured!

Making a Statement

Let's say you're confident that you have the right education, have enough experience, network like a pro, and believe the timing is right, so what do you do next?

Prepare a business plan that includes a clear definition of the product or service that you intend to provide. This exercise will help you think through many of the details that have to happen before you can launch your business. Here are some questions to keep in mind as you draw up your business plan:

• Are there enough customers out there for your product or service? Or is the market saturated?

• Is there a felt need for your product or service? Are you able to provide something that no one else has or at a better price with higher quality?

• How can you differentiate your product or service so that it stands out and performs better than the competition?

• Do you have sufficient capital to launch your idea? If finances get choppy, will your boat continue to float?

• Are you passionate about your entrepreneurial idea? Or are you having doubts?

• Will your product or service contribute to making this world a better place? Or are you in solely for the money? (Not that money isn't important, but money isn't the only thing in life.)

Once your mind is set straight, you can start writing. Think of your plan as a roadmap for your business idea. You want to include the following items in your written plan:

• **An executive summary,** which is a snapshot of your business plan and explains your company's goals.

• **A company description,** which provides additional information and the markets your business serves.

• **A market analysis,** which reveals the research you've done about the competition in your space.

• **A competitor analysis,** which describes your competition and determines how you can differentiate your product or service.

• **An organization and management description,** which outlines the way you'll structure your business.

• **A service or product description,** which describes what you're selling and how you can benefit your customers.

• **A marketing and sales plan,** which explains what you'll do to reach customers.

• **A financial projection,** which shows how you plan to finance your company, your projected sales and expenses, and how you will grow your company.

• **Your unique selling proposition,** which will enable you to stand out from the crowd and show others why you have a winning entrepreneurial idea.

Three Statements to Make

A comprehensive business plan is a lot of work but just the beginning. Once you have a business idea on paper, three important documents should be put into writing and incorporated into your business plan at this stage: the Vision Statement, the Mission Statement, and the Values Statement. Let me describe each one by one.

The **Vision Statement** is a description of what you are all about as a business. The Vision Statement does not have to be very long. Be brief and succinct; the shorter the Vision Statement, the better because your goal is clarity and retention. In many instances, a catchphrase or a sentence or two suffices. You want to be able to remember with a snap of the fingers what your vision is for the company.

Since you can say a lot in a few words, choose your words carefully. The Walt Disney Co. says their goal is to "make people happy." Google states they want to "provide access to the world's information in one click."

A friend of mine in the hospitality business came up with a simple Vision Statement for a resort property he was developing in northern Indiana: "A pleasant experience in the country." That sentence was a reminder that his resort should appeal to urban dwellers in major cities like Chicago and Indianapolis, and Ohio cities like Cincinnati, Cleveland, Columbus, and Toledo. With a beautiful setting in the countryside, my friend knew what direction they wanted to go as they built a hotel, restaurant, gift shop, and petting zoo into a successful enterprise. Everything my friend did was first class, and it showed, thus fulfilling his vision.

Here are several other examples of a Vision Statement:

• Charles Schwab Corporation: "To provide customers with the most useful and ethical financial services in the world."

• Sweetgreen restaurants: "A destination for delicious food that is both healthy for you and aligned with your values."

• H.J. Heinz Company: "Be the world's premier food company, offering nutritious, superior-tasting foods to people everywhere."

And now here are a couple of more altruistic Vision Statements:

• Habitat for Humanity: "A world where everyone has a decent place to live."

• In Touch Ministries: "Proclaiming the Gospel of Jesus Christ to people in every country of the world."

• MEDA (Mennonite Economic Development Associates): "Creating business solutions to poverty."

Let's say you're thinking of starting an e-commerce company. You might have the following Vision Statement: "The right information, the right service, and the right price." A hair salon might go in this direction: "I want your head in my business."

These Vision Statements put a smile on my face.

The next thing to prepare is a **Mission Statement** defining *how* you will fulfill your mission. Similar to Vision Statements, a Mission Statement should be clear, concise, and memorable. Patagonia, an outdoor clothing brand, describes their Mission Statement in this way: "Build the best product, cause no unnecessary harm, use business to inspire, and implement solutions to the environmental crisis."

Jayco, a leader in the recreation vehicle industry, places their Mission Statement front and center on its website landing page: "We will build superior quality and highly valued products. We will treat every situation with the highest level of integrity in a timely manner, and continually work to achieve acceptable returns on our investment."

That's setting the bar high.

The third and—in many ways—the most important document is a **Values Statement**, which defines the values by which you wish to conduct business. Your Values Statement will be instrumental in developing the culture of your organization. Foundational in many ways, a Values Statement is something you're going to want to refer to again and again, especially if you get into an ethical pickle or values conundrum.

Many entrepreneurs are encouraged to put their personal beliefs into their Values Statement, which is a good thing. Your worldview, the way you want to treat people, and the reputation you want to have in the marketplace are incredibly important.

How many times have you heard someone say, "When the new CEO came in, he completely changed the culture of the company" or "Every day we make sure that what we do lines up with the company culture"? They are referring to their Values Statement. I've had the privilege of serving on a family board of directors where the principals developed a Family Values Statement as a cornerstone for their business values. Their statement is also helpful in maintaining a continuity of values across the generations.

One of the businesses I've gone into recently is the hotel industry. Before we broke ground on the Hampton Inn we built in Woodstock, Virginia, I zeroed in on a "caring culture" as the core culture theme for our staff. As part of our Values Statement, I wrote specific guidelines around four main areas of emphasis:

1. Caring for one another.
2. Caring for our guests.
3. Caring for our community.
4. Caring for our environment.

At our employee orientations, I emphasize that we are to always, always, always cover the front desk, twenty-four hours a day, seven days a week because that fulfills our No. 2 goal, "Caring for our guests." As any hotel guest knows, when you enter a hotel or have a question and call the front desk, it's important to have someone on duty, ready to serve.

During the first month of operation, our breakfast hostess arrived at 5 o'clock one morning to prepare the breakfast buffet for our guests. She swung by the front desk. No one was there. She stepped into the office behind the front desk, thinking that our night shift auditor—the front desk person—was doing paperwork or perhaps "resting" his eyelids.

No one there. The office was empty. In other words, there was no one on duty. In fact, she was it—there were no other hotel employees working at the time. Anyone could come through the front doors and make a lot of mischief.

The breakfast hostess knew enough to call our general manager at home and tell her what happened. Of course, our general manager—a woman—was fast asleep when the phone rang, but the startling news set her in motion. Within twenty minutes, she arrived at the hotel sans makeup, but at least we had someone at the front desk who could check out our early departure guests.

Meanwhile, there was no sign of our night auditor, whom I'll call Matt. It was like he disappeared. His car was in the parking lot, however.

About 7:30 that morning, Matt exited a hallway and entered the office behind the front desk. He was sleepy-eyed and rubbing his face to wake up.

"Where have you been?" my general manager asked.

"Sleeping," Matt said.

At least he was honest.

"Sleeping? Where?"

"In one of our rooms."

My general manager dropped her jaw. "What do you mean, 'In one of our rooms?'"

"I don't know how I got there. I don't remember anything. All I know is that I was sleeping and I woke up. I'm sorry about that! I didn't mean to leave the front desk unattended. I'm really sorry it happened."

"And I'm sorry I have to let you go, but you're done," my general manager said. "I'll have a check cut for you today. But go. You're out of here."

My general manager waited until 8 a.m. to call me and report what happened and the action she had taken. I listened, but the entire time I was thinking about a conversation I had with Matt a few days earlier.

"How's the job going?" I asked cheerfully. I am genuinely interested in my employees' welfare.

"Everything's great, Mr. Lefever," replied the courteous young man, who was in his early twenties. "I love my job, but . . ." His voice trailed.

"But what?" I probed.

"But I've never worked a night shift before, which is really screwing me up. I can't sleep when I get home, and then I have some afternoon classes to go to. Consequently, I come to work absolutely bushed and it takes everything within me to keep my eyes open. I'm not getting enough rest, but I'm going to keep trying because I need this job."

I patted him on the shoulder. "If there is anything we can do, you let us know," I said.

And now my general manager was on the line, telling me that she fired Matt for not covering the front desk.

"I'll be in shortly," I said to her.

I met with my general manager and shared with her the conversation I had with Matt. "I would like you to think about our corporate Values Statement," I said to her. "Our No. 1 objective is 'Caring for one another.' This young man made a mistake. There's no doubt about that. But how could we, as a company, care for him in a situation like this? I'd like you to think that through and ask yourself if your decision to let him go fits with our values in this situation."

My general manager nodded. "I will do that, Mr. Lefever."

She decided to call Matt back to discuss how the incident happened. Once she heard him describe how difficult it was for him to keep his eyes open in the wee hours of the morning, she decided to give him a second chance. I was pleased to hear about her decision—as a rule, I don't like to overrule decisions made in the field—and Matt returned to work and became an outstanding employee for a number of years.

That was a happy ending, but another values situation still gives me angst today. It happened when I failed to carefully think through my values as it related to a specific business opportunity—financing auto loans.

Here's what happened. Back when I was working for High Industries, we invested some excess cash to a sub-prime lending broker in Austin, Texas. He was quite an operator, lending money to various loan companies that specialized in sub-prime financing for car buyers and then rolling them into a bond and securitizing them. What we learned was that the rapid turnover of sub-prime loans can be pretty lucrative. (A sub-prime loan is made to borrowers who have poor credit and a greater risk of defaulting, but they pay a lot more in interest to get the loan since traditional lenders will not lend them money.)

One day I thought, "Why don't we do this ourselves? We don't need a loan broker in Austin who's taking a big cut."

I happened to run into a guy who had started a lending division for Xerox and told him about my idea. He said he was on board. Then we put a business plan together, which I presented to my boss, Dale High. "Go for it," he said.

The next step was hiring two high-powered guys to be our senior management team: one was running Ford Motor Credit, and the other guy was assistant treasurer for Texas Instruments. So we had three well-qualified executives on our team.

High Industries put in most of the money—millions! Then we went to eight large banks and said we would take the auto loan applications of the people they didn't want because they were too much of a credit risk. These were known in the trade as sub-prime borrowers. What these means in plainer English is that they were poor, often working-class people who needed transportation desperately enough to pay up to 18 percent interest on their monthly auto loan.

Our business plan was to build up the loan portfolio, get it rated by Moody's, Fitch, or Standard & Poor's, and then flip it for a profit. No muss, no fuss.

In January 1996, we were processing three-year, five-year, and seven-year auto loans. We had around 3,000 loans on the books. The average auto loan was $12,000.

For some reason, the computer we were using didn't kick out the monthly bills for the five-year loans that January. (It actually was a Y2K computer glitch.) We didn't catch the mistake for two months, meaning we had two months of loans that we weren't getting paid on. Human nature being what it is, if people don't get a statement in the mail, they don't pay.

Suddenly, we had to send statements in March asking for payment of the last three months. For many working class families, that was money already spent. Many didn't have three months' worth of auto loan payments sitting in a bank account.

So they didn't pay.

Do you know what happens when you don't pay your auto loan?

Right—your car gets repossessed.

When I heard that the Repo Man was out in full force, taking away poor people's transportation in the middle of the night, my heart sank. This was a nasty business that I no longer wanted to be a part of. The whole premise of helping working-class families obtain a car disappeared.

Our auto loan business no longer fit with one of my cherished values, which was "Treat all persons with dignity." We were treating a class of less-fortunate people poorly in a system that almost set them up for failure.

When our late payment percentage spiked, our credit rating also went south in a hurry. That development, coupled with the havoc we were inflicting on people's lives when their cars were repossessed, prompted us to get out of the sub-prime auto loan business. We sold our company to a bottom-feeder and licked our wounds.

That was a bad situation all the way around.

The stories like the ones I just shared are why I believe the Values Statement is often the most important—and most over-looked—part of starting a business. A Values Statement is like a first impression because it's a lasting impression. You often only have one chance to establish your company culture, so you want to get it aligned right from the very beginning.

A company culture is often overlooked or treated as a step-child. One of the leading executive leadership management programs at Harvard's Executive Business School has an easy-to-remember 4+2 formula that includes the company's culture.

When starting a business, the Harvard Executive Business School recommends that you need all four of the following:

- Strategy
- Execution
- Culture
- Structure

And then you need at least two of the following:

- Talent
- Leadership
- Innovation
- Monitoring and assessment

Regarding the last four bullet points, your start-up company can succeed if you have innovative, talented employees and noth-ing else or strong leadership with continual monitoring and assessment without the talent employees, but if you don't have a company culture, you're going to have problems.

Bottom line: pay close attention to your Values Statement and establish a culture within the company from day one.

Getting Down to Brass Tacks

I'd like to say a few things about developing the right key strategies when starting a business. Since strategy refers to how you're going to implement your master plan, here are some important questions to consider:

• Who will be my target customer? (This is critical since once you've identified your customer, then, as Amazon says, you become "obsessed" over that customer.)

• What is it about my product or service that will be unique and compelling for my target customer?

• What channels will be the most efficient and effective in reaching my target customer?

• How will I position my product or service—low-cost or high quality?

• Are there operating procedures that I can implement to reinforce my uniqueness to my target customer?

• What can I do to enhance the marketing and sales functions?

• How can I integrate my key strategies to maximize my chances for success?

Here's what an integrated strategy for a start-up food service company where I was part of senior management looked like. First of all, we decided that our business plan should serve mid- to large-size companies within a fifty-mile radius of our cooking and manufacturing facility with superior quality food, delivered primarily to vending machines on site. We would also meet any catering needs of our clients.

Since we were basing our differentiation on our ability to offer fresher and better-quality food we asked ourselves: How were we going to do that?

As we looked at our procedures—cooking the meats, preparing the vegetables and breads, and making the sandwiches—we decided that if we were going to have fresher food than our competition, then we had to make those sandwiches and salads as late as possible before delivery.

We knew that a key competitor made their sandwiches and salads twelve to fifteen hours before delivery, which meant their food products sat in a refrigerator for a long time before delivery. Our key competitor was more than a fifty-mile radius from their customers.

We decided to do several things to differentiate ourselves. The first was to stay within a fifty-mile radius, as I mentioned. The next—and most important—thing we started was a late-evening shift from 9 p.m. to 4 a.m. to produce the sandwiches and salads, which were loaded directly onto the trucks for delivery. We also sourced the very best ingredients we could find since everyone can taste quality.

So quality ingredients, a night shift for production, and tightened-up supply chain would re-enforce our quality goal in a tangible way.

With such a unique operating procedure in place, our sales people had a story to tell when they met with new companies. They could explain *how* and *why* our sandwiches and salads were better.

But did they *taste* better? In that case, we offered to do a blind test of our products in the employee lunchroom with their current vendor or any other company they were thinking of bringing in.

"Let the employees vote," our sales reps would say to the Human Resources department. They usually handled matters like what food to offer employees during their breaks. We knew we'd get a good turnout because who turns down a free meal these days?

I like to think that these food competitions were as one-sided as Tom Brady and the New England Patriots playing against a high school team. We would win those blind taste-testing contests every time, hands down. And when company employees pointed to our sandwiches and salads as the ones they wanted, the HR department wasn't going to disappoint them.

Notice an interesting aspect of this integrated operation-and-sales approach: We hadn't mentioned price yet to these companies! Because we won a blind taste test with the rank-and-file employees, and the HR person wanted to be responsive to the wishes of their associates, this enhanced our ability to charge an extra 10 percent for the much-improved food quality. In many cases, we offered more food choices, made possible by our tighter turnaround, and thus longer shelf life in the vending machines. We usually got the business, and the employees were happy with their improved food options.

This story illustrates the importance of strategizing. Strategy, like an annual plan, needs to be a "living" document. Change happens all the time: technology breakthroughs occur, consumer preferences may change (for instance, far more people are health conscious about what they eat today), new competitors may enter the picture, the economic picture may change, or a crisis may impact your business. Be sure to regularly evaluate the relevancy of your strategy and the way your entrepreneurial idea will approach business.

In effect, strategic planning tries to answer the question of how your firm will operate and be competitive. A good strategy that is implemented well leads to building an organization with a sustainable competitive advantage.

While there are many different strategic options and marketing positions to consider, here are five generic options:

1. A low-cost strategy targets price-sensitive buyers. Examples: Walmart, Southwest Airlines, and Dollar Tree.

2. A focused niche and low-cost strategy targets those interested in a brand company, but at a low cost. Examples: McDonalds, Pizza Hut, and Chevy.

3. A best-value strategy targets value-conscience buyers. Examples: Dell, Target, and Toyota.

4. A focused niche and differentiation strategy targets unique higher-price buyers willing to pay for quality. Examples: Starbucks, BMW, and Mercedes.

5. A brand differentiation strategy targets customers who desire a unique or status product. Examples: Nike, Rolex, and Volvo (for their safety).

Where you do you see yourself? Once you determine the best positioning for your product or service, you can work on the best strategy to turn your business into a success.

After strategy comes plans for executing details, starting with hiring. Right up front, I want to say a word about what your hiring practices should be, even if you don't foresee hiring any employees in the foreseeable future. Nonetheless, it's never too early to be thinking about developing a hiring process and learning the questions you'll need to ask during the interviewing process. It's imperative to find men and women aligned with your values, competent at the position you're looking to fill, and sharing a passion for your entrepreneurial company.

For example, at Chick-fil-A, the human resources department relies on the "Three Big C's" when interviewing an applicant:

• Character

- Competency
- Chemistry

If any one of those is out of whack, you're not going to be happy with that hire.

Last Thought

Remember, you're the captain of the ship. As you get ready to launch, you may see the need to hire a first mate or crew member. You'll need a strong team behind you to help you weather the storms that are sure to come.

Now a practical suggestion on a launching technique. You may have a good job, or it may be unwise to leave your current employment and risk it all on an idea that may not be successful.

In such a situation, my suggestion is that you test the waters by working on your entrepreneurial business in the evenings or on weekends while maintaining your current job. You might think of yourself as a "part-time entrepreneur." This greatly reduces your start-up risk, enabling you to maintain the cash flow from your current job while testing your idea.

The lesson to be learned: you need to be thoughtful about the best strategy to get started because you only get to launch once.

So imagine pushing away from the dock and entering the harbor. You're heading for the open seas, and you better be ready for some big waves—or white water!

THREE

Getting Wet

"'I can't do it' never accomplished anything. 'I will try' has accomplished wonders."
—George Burnham, civic leader and U.S. Congressman
in the 1930s

"A man's reach should be further than his grasp."
—Robert Browning, 19th century English poet

"Be fearless but not reckless."
—Allon Lefever, author of *Launching the Entrepreneur Ship*

J ust as it takes a weekend sailor many months, if not years, to refurbish a boat in dry-dock, it could take you just as long to write a business plan, analyze the competition in your market, outline a marketing and sales plan, work out financial projections, and toil on a Values Statement. You'll also have to identify key people you want to hire when you launch your business or pick out a retail outlet or office space.

All these agenda items have to be in motion before you can lower your craft into the water and determine if your entrepreneurial idea is seaworthy. But as any weekend sailor knows, the first stop is filling up the gas tank, means a significant outlay of cash. You can count on experiencing start-up costs when you test the waters with your entrepreneurial idea or business.

Your start-ups costs could be significant, or they can be of the shoestring variety, depending on what you're planning to do. Either way, where are you going to get the money required to launch? Every business, no matter how big or how small, will have capital working requirements. Starting a business without enough cash for the first few months—an entire year is better—is like heading out of the harbor with a gas tank that's on empty. Not only will you not get very far, but you could be set adrift and eventually crash against the shoals.

I can assure you: the start-up phase to any business idea will take longer than expected and require more investment dollars than you originally assumed. This is why it's critical to have the money side figured out before you set sail.

I think you should have some of your own money—your hard-fought savings—invested directly into your company. Having skin in the game reminds you that you're risking a lot. Investing your own money allows you to retain 100 percent equity in your company, but if you bring in investors, their comfort level and their confidence will rise if your greenbacks are on the line as well.

I certainly saw the value of commitment when I invested in Rod's idea to start an Internet Service Provider in the Lancaster area. I was at a stage in my career where I could easily write a $10,000 check, but for Rod, who was fresh out of MBA school, ten grand was like pushing all of his poker chips into the center of a felt table. He was "all in" because $10,000 tapped him out.

It's okay to make a calculated risk, but you don't want to gamble. The great World War II general Erwin Rommel once made a distinction between the two. A risk and a gamble both involve boldness, he said, but the difference is that with a gamble, you could lose your life. With a risk, you can recover if you lose.

Gambling in the business world, however, means that a failure could send you into a financial and personal tailspin that ends up costing you everything. It could destroy you, leaving behind plenty of collateral damage. That's why I say be fearless but not reckless.

It's essential to estimate how much cash you will need to launch your business idea. After you tap your personal resources, the typical people to approach are any family members who have the financial means and the necessary interest to support your idea. This is what Rod and a million other entrepreneurs commonly do. You might find some family members who are willing to lend you the money and not necessarily take an equity stake in the company as long as they are eventually repaid. Their main concern may be repayment.

Next you might seek out persons interested in your specific product or service. These investors could be friends or acquaintances. They might be interested because of the mission or the cause you represent (especially if your idea is in the social entrepreneurship arena), or they believe your concept has money-making potential. Or, as we see with the five sharks on *Shark Tank*, they want to invest in a segment of the market they like, like Mark Cuban with tech apps or Lori Greiner with companies that produce household products like Squatty Potty or Phone Soap that she can readily sell on QVC.

These types of financial backers are often referred to as "angel" investors. Their capital may be a one-time investment to help propel your business idea forward or an ongoing injection of money to support and carry your entrepreneurial idea through the difficult start-up period until you get your sea legs.

Angel investors are more patient and not as demanding as pure venture capitalists, also known as VCs, since they are investing in you—the entrepreneur—as well as the viability of the business. They are often affluent individuals willing to take a chance on you by injecting capital into your start-up in exchange for ownership equity or company debt. Your financing will usually be a combination of debt and equity.

The flip side of the investor coin are the venture capitalists, aka the "sharks." Drawing from pooled money collected from other investors and definitely in the game to make money, they can feel like razor-toothed sharks circling their mark. VCs are looking for investment opportunities where they can earn a massive return on their money if the entrepreneurial business takes off. Silicon Valley's Peter Thiel's investment of $500,000 in Mark Zuckerberg back in 2004, when he was set on turning his dorm-room project into a website called Facebook, is a classic example. Thiel's investment in Facebook in the early days turned out to be worth more than $1 billion in cash.

For every Peter Thiel or Chris Sacca, an early investor in Twitter and ride-share company Uber and part-time host shark on *Shark Tank*, there are thousands of venture capitalists who see their investment dollars go up in smoke. Because of the home-run-or-strike-out volatility, venture capitalists demand a bigger slice of your company than angel investors would ask.

Depending on the size of your capital requirements, you may need to seek out professional venture capital firms. They do not suffer fools gladly: seeking money at this level will absolutely require an airtight, well-written business plan, a strong financial presentation, résumés of key managers, and five-year and ten-year projections.

You could also seek a bank loan, but bankers and investment bankers are not interested in investing in companies during the launch phase. If traditional brick-and-mortar banks are to make an investment at all, that would come after there is a sound track record of performance.

Your final option is seeking out "public money" through an IPO, or initial public offering. In my experience, this option will be practically impossible since you have no balance sheet or profit-and-loss statement to build your case with Wall Street financiers.

Money on Hand

I'd like to share two personal examples of the importance of having an equal amount of sufficient cash and perseverance on hand at start-up time:

The first example relates to the Hampton Inn that I own in Woodstock, Virginia.

When you build a hotel, you want to open at the beginning of your best season, to get a nice start on occupancy and cash flow. That's on page one of the Hotel 101 playbook.

I planned the start of my hotel project and all the related construction schedules so that we would open by April 2009, ready for the strong summer season. As we began the site work, even with the necessary permits in hand, we ran into an unanticipated issue with the Environmental Protection Agency (EPA) related to the storm water runoff. (Yes, I was one of those entrepreneurs who ran afoul of government regulatory rules that hamstring small, medium, and large businesses, which is to say *all* business start-ups.)

I huddled up with our planning engineers who informed me that they were uncertain if the runoff problem would result in the need to change the site plan. On the side of caution, we halted excavation and site work—and waited around to deal with the EPA. The bureaucrats took their sweet time getting around to us, which resulted in a three-month delay to resolve the issue. By the time earthmoving equipment was back on the site, we were well into the winter mud season—the most unfavorable time to build a large hotel. It was impossible to make up the lost time.

Our Hampton Inn opened after Labor Day, when kids were back in school and families had stopped traveling to the Shenandoah Valley of Virginia. In addition, we were in the midst of the Great Recession in 2009, and the local hotel market was off 17 percent from the forecast of a third-party feasibility study we had done *before* the housing bubble popped in 2008.

So when you combine starting construction at the wrong time of the year and an unanticipated recession, we had to work very hard, raise more cash for working capital, and really control our costs. Day by day, week by week, and month by month we persisted and made it through the rapids. I was grateful, especially because I knew that a competitor only twenty miles away from our hotel gave up under similar circumstances and had to file bankruptcy. He lost his hotel.

A second example happened when I was working at High Industries back in the 1980s. Actually, the story has a bit of a *Shark Tank* flavor because it started when I was asked to drop in on a "venture forum" in Harrisburg, where entrepreneurs gathered to make pitches for money.

Remember, this was at a time in my career when I was a senior vice president who ran various businesses for High Industries, so I was on the lookout for interesting and profitable investment opportunities.

A couple of computer whizzes stood up and talked about how the CD-ROM market was coming on strong and that they were using the latest computer and robot technology to serve this emerging industry. This was at a time when music and movies were moving rapidly from cassette tape—remember videocassettes?—to compact discs, so I had a cursory understanding of what was happening. I mean, who wanted to mess with bulky videocassettes or cassette tapes that car players ate up regularly when a small, portable, round disc made of molded polymer could digitally store and play back audio music and video movies?

I looked at their business plan. I didn't understand the terminology but I got the general gist of what was going on: their plan was to utilize the latest technology and robots to help achieve efficient smaller volume runs typical of CD-ROM.

They believed they could do changeovers quickly and efficiently, and thus be a lower-cost producer for smaller production runs, creating a niche for their company since a typical manufacturing plant was designed for high-volume, long-run music. Those CD-ROM manufacturers couldn't turn their production facilities on a dime like we thought we could.

When I walked through the business plan with Dale High, my boss, he said, "I don't think this is for us. It's pretty high tech, and we don't understand that. I'm not sure if what they say about the CD-ROM business is going to happen."

We passed, but then two months later, I returned to Harrisburg for the venture forum, and those two tech wizards had a new, improved business plan. One of the guys told me he had been an audio engineer for singer Billy Joel and helped cut his first CD album using the latest recording technology. He also dropped the name of Barbra Streisand and how she was a client. He reiterated that they were on to something and had gone back and reworked their proposal. Was I interested in seeing it again?

I said sure, and this time the picture became clearer. Dale's interest ticked up. The opportunity was there to make tens of millions of dollars. "We need to look at this more closely," he said.

Dale green-lighted a $30,000 study performed by the best tech geek firm we could find. We learned who the players were, what the competition was like, the sales projections, and what growth rates we could expect. The positive report gave us the little push we needed to start a new company called American Helix, which, at the time, became the only company in the world making CDs in a manufacturing cell based on electric molding machines, interconnected by robots.

With our investment dollars, the American Helix's high-tech plant ramped up to two production lines. The plant production start-up was just as we planned and we were pleased with its performance, but then two huge problems hit simultaneously: the rate of growth for CD-ROMs was not materializing as we expected, and the selling price of CDs fell quickly to only about two-thirds of where it had been and where we had forecasted it to be.

We knew American Helix had to scramble if we were going to reach a break-even level of production. Putting feelers out in our industry, we sought out the best markets we could find, which were the smaller music record labels that needed shorter production runs that fit into our efficient changeover plant design vs. the bigger operators.

That was all good, but then the second huge problem stared us in the face: the selling price of music CDs, given the high volumes, was only half the price level of CD-ROM discs, meaning we would receive less revenue on each music disc. We gradually acquired more of the smaller record label business, but even at full capacity, our plant was running below breakeven at the lower price level. It appeared, however, that we could at least break even if we added a third production line (at little additional overhead cost), and we had the building space for a third production line. If we could further improve our efficiency from our third line, we could turn a profit.

Singer John Denver accepted our invitation to watch his Earth Songs CD being manufactured inside our American Helix CD plant in 1990. With us is David Dering, president of American Helix.

Fortunately, High Industries was in a position to take the risk and provide the capital to support another $1.5 million-dollar line of credit for equipment that would expand output with a third line of production. It took a lot of work, but we persisted and made it through those rapids and enjoyed several profitable years. Then the Japanese company, Kao, came along and bought us for our world-class technology and superior quality.

The lesson to be learned here?

Be sure to have sufficient capital resources and persistence to get you through the start-up turbulence . . . and keep your boat financially afloat.

Building a Brand

Believe it or not, one of the most overlooked items is deciding on a name for your company. You can't start "building a brand" if you haven't come up with a clever moniker for your company.

You can hire a "naming firm" that employs linguists and uses proprietary computer programs to come up with potential names, or go to websites like brandbucket.com to purchase a brand name, but that costs precious cash. You'd be better off brainstorming with friends and family . . . throwing out names and seeing if any of them stick. Or even better, test some potential name ideas with your target customer group and obtain their feedback.

Company names fall into five categories:

1. Coined names. It's getting more and more difficult to find words in the dictionary that haven't already been used to name a business. Creating a new word to describe your business has been a popular way to go and certainly works for companies like Accenture and Zillow. You see car manufacturers dip into the coined word basket all the time: they name their car models Altima, Aerio, Azera, Amnati, Aveo . . . and that's just the first letter of the alphabet.

Coined names have to be short, easy to pronounce, and roll off the tongue. You can combine names like GoDaddy or RiteAid or fuse syllables like Logomatics or Unitrics. You can make up your own words: believe it or not, Sony, Häagen-Dazs, Ikea, and Google are incredible examples.

2. Descriptive names. When we wanted to start our ISP company, we chose a name that described what we did: SuperNet Interactive Services. Combining two nouns into one word, like SuperNet, was a cutting-edge idea twenty-five years ago. You still see the practice done today—GoDaddy being a prime example— but it's rapidly becoming passé.

The downside to descriptive names is that they can be bland and fail to make an impression in social media or paid advertising. A company called Computer Associates or Springtime Flowers wouldn't move the needle.

3. Abstract names. These are real words that have no obvious connection to the business that's being launched. Viewed as blanks slates by the public the first time they hear the name, their value comes from their quirkiness. What did you think when you heard someone tell you that they bought something on "Amazon." You didn't know what to think, right? Now we all know the word *Amazon* so well that you never associate the word with its origin, which is as the name of the largest river in the world, located in South America.

4. Acronyms. Ever been to CVS? Of course you have, but I'm sure you don't know that the initials are an abbreviation for Consumer Values Stores. Nonetheless, acronyms are popular choices for company names. We went this route when we merged our ISP with Denver and Ephrata Telephone Co. and called ourselves D&E SuperNet.

Some companies start out with regular-sounding name that gets shortened to an acronym. The Columbia Broadcasting System and Federal Express are known around the world as CBS and FedEx today. The downside to using an abbreviation is that they often lack an emotional appeal, letters can be easily transposed, and can sound a lot like other company names.

5. Founders' or partners' names. You see this all the time with law firms. The Los Angeles entertainment law firm of Ziffren, Brittenham, Branca, Fischer, Gilbert-Lurie, Stiffelman, Cook, Johnson, Lande & Wolf holds the world's record for longest law firm name ever.

The problem is that companies evolve over time as some of the principals either leave the firm for greener pastures or retire or—gasp—die. One of the great ministries of the 20th century was the Billy Graham Evangelistic Association, but what will happen to the ministry when Billy, who's nearing one hundred—receives his reward in heaven?

Once you decide on a name for your company, you need to get cracking on a logo. Logos are a critical aspect of marketing your business because this graphical representation anchors your brand in customer's minds. Where would Nike and Starbucks be today without the "swoosh" on their shoes, packaging, and advertising or the 16th century Norse mermaid on every cup of Starbucks java? McDonald's without its golden arches?

Be aware that design and colors of your logo come alive on the web and with social media. I once had a logo for U.S. Internet Providers that looked absolutely fine on letterhead, but when we used it on our website, it looked flat and uninspiring. We changed our logo so that it popped online, which is even more important today since every new business needs an online presence today.

That's where people's eyeballs are fixed, right?

Maiden Voyage

You've got capital, a great name, and a nice logo. You launch your business, but it doesn't take long for you to figure out that this is no holiday cruise. I tell entrepreneurs that the first few months in business are often quite frustrating and challenging as you try to find your way.

Expect Murphy's Law to strike every day because what can go wrong will go wrong. You can expect unanticipated delays in receiving product, vendor quality issues, shortages in the supply chain, purchase orders that were never fulfilled, and steep learning curves for your staff. Those are what I call internal issues—to do items that theoretically you can control.

Other aggravations will be more of the external variety, such as how a competitor in your space reacts to your entry into her market. You may see that the market acceptance of your product or service is far slower than you expected or projected, governmental regulations were more than you bargained for—and far costlier—or rising interest rates just increased your cost of doing business. Start-up companies are greatly impacted by how the national economy is doing.

A successful entrepreneur will put everything he has at his disposal into resolving these challenges. That often means working smart, then hard, and putting in the long hours. When navigating through rough waters, a steady hand is needed at the helm—and you might be the only person with the knowledge of where you want your ship of commerce to go or how to get there. Persistence is a virtue.

I don't want to characterize the business world as a jungle, but it is survival of the fittest as the market has a way of weeding out poor performers. That's the mechanism of natural selection because as an idea, product, or service matures, competition will reward those with the best practices, the best strategy, and the best execution.

People forget that before the start of the 20th century, you either walked, rode a horse, or took a train to where you wanted to go. Then "horseless carriages" came along in the late 1800s, powered by steam, combustion, and electrical motors. The combustion engine eventually beat out the competition because early American automobile pioneers like Ransom E. Olds and Henry Ford built reliable combustion engines and rejected steam— because there was a risk of boiler explosion—and electrical— because batteries were in their infancy and couldn't move a car with much speed or over a long distance—power from the start.

Olds and Ford weren't the only two entrepreneurs racing to get their automobiles to market. Did you know that between 1904 and 1908—the length of a presidential term—that there were 241 automobile manufacturing firms in the United States? One of those start-ups was the Ford Motor Company, which opened its factory in June 1903 and sold its first car several weeks later on June 23, 1903. (Try that Tesla!)

At one point, there were over five hundred automobile makers in the early 1900s—many of them mom-and-pop entrepreneurs hand-making beautiful automobiles in their backyard barns. And then along came Henry Ford who figured out how to make an assembly line and crank out Model T roadsters by the thousands each day. Ford's revolutionary assembly-line manufacturing techniques drove down the cost of the Model T—by cutting the man hours to produce a car by 75 percent—to a price point that the average American family could afford to buy a "Tin Lizzie."

Those backyard mom-and-pops? They shuttered and jumpstarted a trend of consolidation to where there are just four major U.S. companies making cars today: Ford, General Motors, Chrysler, and Tesla, along with minor players like Faraday Future and Fisker, who make electric cars.

I saw market forces at work during my decade in the ISP world. At its height in the late 1990s, there were over 5,000 ISP's (Internet Service Providers) in the US. Nearly twenty years later, only a small fraction of those 5,000 exist today. The joke is that you can pick any ISP you want, as long as it's Comcast, Cox, or Spectrum (Time-Warner).

So, are you seeking to do business in an area of the market that is expanding to fill a demand or contracting because the big fish are gobbling up the minnows?

Those are the questions you need to be asking as you get ready to launch.

FOUR

Finding the Right Channel Out of the Harbor

"Progress is the activity of today, and the assurance of tomorrow."
—Ralph Waldo Emerson, 19th century poet

"I thatched my roof when the sun was shining, and now I'm not afraid of the storm."
—George F. Stivers, American businessman

"If you don't know where you're going, you might not get there."
—Yogi Berra, New York Yankee baseball legend

You've decided to loosen the tie lines and launch your business.

In the old days, that meant hanging up an "Open for Business" poster in a storefront window and seeing who walked through the front door. While you may be leasing space in a brick-and-mortar building, it's more likely that your business resides on the Internet, where literally billions of people can find you with a few clicks.

If and when you decide to launch your business, let me put a little wind in your sails: according to the U.S. Bureau of Labor, 75 percent of new business survive the first year and 69 percent are still viable after the first two years. The number of successful businesses drops to 50 percent after five years, however, which speaks to the importance of continuous planning and reviewing after you launch your business.

For the purposes of this chapter, let's focus on the first year of your business launch. This is where you need to pay close attention to your Annual Plan. Ask yourself these questions:

- What are your expectations for revenue and expenses during your first year?
- Do you have enough capital on hand?
- How fast are you burning through capital?
- What's a realistic timeframe for sales and profitability?

To return to a maritime scenario, a business launch is often leaving the dock and motoring slowly through a harbor. Are you heading in the right direction? Do you have all the necessary provisions on board? Use this time to check your gauges before you reach more turbulent waters. Make sure your marketing and social media efforts are lined up and ready to go.

You—as the captain of the ship—need to do an attitude check as you motor along. The biggest thing I've seen over the years is that entrepreneurs tend to be overly optimistic and generally expect sales to be much higher than they turn out to be. They're saying to themselves, *Once people see my product on the Internet, they'll love it and order right away,* but the reality is that customers generally need a couple of stages of evaluation before they make their first purchase. They may want to read reviews from customers who have something to say about your product or service before ordering. Until this happens, the sales you were expecting in the first quarter may not happen until your third quarter—if at all.

When I work with entrepreneurs, I try to tamp down their expectations for the first year. They think they may sell 20,000 widgets, but I try to get them down to 15,000. Sure, 20,000 units would be wonderful, but if they expense for 20,000 and only sell 10,000 units, they could be in trouble in a hurry. Revenue has a way of never matching expectations.

I once helped a young couple start a private school that was based on the Waldorf philosophy—a way of teaching young children that was similar to the Montessori method. A Waldorf education does not include media of any kind (no computers, tablets, or electronics) and tries to teach children how to think—not *what* to think. All in all, a worthy educational goal.

Let's call this couple James and Judy, who were childless and passionate about teaching the Waldorf method. A church in their hometown of Harrisonburg, Virginia, was excited about what they were trying to do, so they were able to secure classroom facilities at a reasonable cost.

While this was a team effort, James planned to keep his day job in information technology while Judy left a full-time job to run the school. I thought that James staying with his job was a good idea because they needed at least one paycheck coming in during their first school year.

According to their Annual Plan, they planned on twenty kids enrolling the first year, which would make the numbers work. When their Waldorf school opened up in the fall, however, only six children enrolled, meaning their revenue was about one-third of what they expected. Judy had to work for no salary. To pay a much-needed assistant, they reached into their own pockets. Had James quit his job, they would have experienced serious financial hurt.

The first year, as you would expect, was a real struggle. But Judy persevered and gained respect. The parents of their six students told others about what a great learning experience their children had during the school year. Based on the positive word-of-mouth, twenty students enrolled for their second year, which gave them real traction in the academic world.

Another time, I helped an entrepreneur named Randy get started in the production of components that were part of the supply chain for the recreational vehicle industry in Elkhart, Indiana. Randy rented a half-decent facility, purchased the necessary machinery, and landed a nice contract with one of the operators in that market. You couldn't ask for a better launch.

Within a year, Randy and his team were knocking out very good products at a very fair price. In Randy's case, business grew faster than expected. They needed more facilities, more machinery, and more labor, so they had to scurry to secure additional capital.

My entrepreneur knew he had a winner. Randy's attitude shifted from "Are we going to survive?" to "We have a winner here, so how do we plan for the potential that's here in terms of the additional capacity and the additional capital that's going to be required?"

Randy had to adjust his Annual Plan so he could ramp up production in the short term. Randy understood that he had been handed an unusual opportunity and needed to make hay while the sun shone brightly. He had to think about how big a building the company had to move into. Fortunately for him, a strong start meant additional financing would be easier to find.

My point is if you're not thinking about Phase 2 until you're out of capacity and can't serve your customer, you're going to miss a huge opportunity.

Life's a Risk

I'm the first to acknowledge that every business is different with varying levels of product life cycles and vastly different obsolescence timelines.

No single template fits every business, and you have to expect the unexpected. When we were building our SuperNet Internet service provider business, I was surprised how quickly the Cisco routers improved every six months. Consequently, we were careful not to make huge purchases of new routers because the longer we waited, the better chance we had to buy improved, faster routers—for less money—the next time we needed to expand our network.

I found out the hotel business was different. I learned that if we invested in a well-structured design for the hotel and put money into employee training on the front end, our hotel could get on a roll for many years without having to invest a ton of additional capital. Sure, I knew our computer systems would become obsolete after so many years, but if we did proper maintenance, we could focus our energies on driving more business to the front lobby.

So where are you right now—especially if you've put your boat into the water and have officially launched your business?

First, evaluate if your overall culture is healthy. I'm a big believer in reviewing the Values Statement early on to ensure that you're living up to your stated values. Your Values Statement is a refreshing reminder about what you are and what you hold dear in terms of company values. Your employees will notice and sense that you care.

If you refer early on to your Values Statement as you develop your marketing efforts and/or your personnel policies, you will be well served. At SuperNet, we decided from the outset that we were going to maintain good customer service, which is why we made the commitment to have six customers for each modem, or a ratio of 6:1. When we exploded with growth, it would have been easy to let that number slip to 8:1 because it would have saved us the cost of buying more modems, but such a move would have taken us from our value of superior customer service.

Think of what happened to AOL when they made their move to offer unlimited access to the Internet. They didn't have enough modems to support that effort, so customers got a lot of busy signals. In the Lancaster area, word got around: *Switch to SuperNet if you don't want a busy signal.*

Because of our company value for top-notch customer service, we had gained a strong reputation in southeastern Pennsylvania, which reminds me of what the wisest man who ever lived—Solomon—once wrote: "Choose a good reputation over great riches; being held in high esteem is better than silver or gold."

You must be willing to maintain your company values, even if it's going to cost you silver and gold. That's the way we decided to look at the hotel business. The Hampton brand has a policy, which we endorsed, that if our Hampton Inn customers weren't 100 percent satisfied, they could get all of their money back. The refunds hurt, but you know what? Our money-back guarantee made the staff work hard to make sure that didn't happen.

Most of our Hampton Inn refunds occurred because of noise—a cranky air conditioning unit was too loud all night or maybe our indoor swimming pool was overcrowded because we opened it up to a kiddy birthday party for a local family.

In 2015, we issued 107 refunds for hotel stays. In 2016, there were 101 free nights. That may sound like a lot, but that's out of around 32,000 room nights, or a percentage of .003, meaning that one out of every 317 room nights was comped. I can live with those numbers.

Occasionally, we have someone who abuses the system to get a free room, but that happens very seldom. With a 100 percent satisfaction guarantee, our employees know they have to do everything they can to please the guest. If an air conditioner starts screeching and we don't get it fixed in time, causing our next guest to complain, then it's on our front desk staff because we shouldn't have that problem. Bottom line: our money-back guarantee helps everyone get aligned in what we want to do. Our refund policy also creates positive online reviews.

Sometimes external risk and internal risk management can overlap. For example, be aware that the World Wide Web can be a two-edged sword when it comes to online reviews. I've heard multiple businesses owners complain about websites like Yelp and Angie's List, which are hugely popular with Millennials because they publish crowd-sourced reviews of local businesses. According to a survey by Dimensional Research, an overwhelming 90 percent of respondents said their buying decisions were influenced by online reviews. Do your best to stay current on what social media is saying about your product or service, and respond accordingly.

Oh, I wonder if that new Thai restaurant is any good? I think I'll check Yelp.

The problem is that plenty of business owners over the years have said that Yelp marketers call up their businesses and offer to get rid of nasty reviews in exchange for advertising dollars—a lot of them.

What's happening out there can be pretty insidious. You'll serve yourself best by doing the best job you can so as to generate positive reviews. Part of your online strategy means creating the best website you can within your budget. If people find your website but believe your overall presentation is amateurish or convoluted, they will click on to something else in a nanosecond.

Not only does your website have to be easy to navigate, but the photography has to be first-class. Clear, crisp, and engaging photography can make or break a website. You want to attract eyeballs with gorgeous photos so that people will say "Wow" and stay with you. Snapshot-quality photography will lose you customers as well as credibility.

Hire professionals—or friends with excellent photography equipment who'll charge you less—to produce interesting and captivating photos of your service or product. Give those photos prominence on your website.

I'm on the board of a fairly large furniture company that does a lot of e-commerce. They purchased a large rotating platform so they can give customers a chance to see the product from every angle. This company invested their money wisely in good photography, and their Internet sales are exploding.

People are visual. If your website has too much wording or not enough visual elements, then the page won't grab potential customers. Technical information should come after an additional click. Keep things fairly simple: show customers the product six different ways and then give them an easy opportunity to click through for details.

If you have a catchy YouTube video, leverage that by asking your social media friends to post on their Facebook page or pass it along to their friends. Maybe your product or service can go "viral," resulting in a ton of unexpected sales.

That's the good side to online marketing.

The bad side is that no one might ever find you on the Internet. Around 140,000 new websites are launched *every day*, or more than 51 million every year.

That's why it's important to keep tabs on your Internet traffic. Learning how to maximize SEO (search engine optimization) and other Internet marketing tactics is the name of the game today. It's also key to regularly review your Annual Plan and Strategic Plan. When I began my career, many larger companies would develop Strategic Plans over a five-to-ten-year period, but I've seen this aspect of planning change over the years because of how *fast* business evolves these days. Now I recommend three-to-five-year Strategic Plans.

It's amazing how quickly things change. I hold up as Exhibit A the casual dining chain Chipotle, which was a huge success with a menu of burritos and salad bowls made with higher-grade chicken and fresh, cut-on-premises vegetables. In 2015, however, several employees failed to wash their hands or came to work sick, and there was an outbreak of norovirus, salmonella, and E. coli that was traced back to their restaurants in Minnesota, Southern California, Washington, and Oregon. The nationwide media jumped on the story. Chipotle's stock tanked, and even today, the casual dining chain is still recovering from the series of food safety problems.

Because stuff happens, your Annual Plan and your three-to-five-year Strategic Plan need to be "living documents," flexible and responsive to marketplace changes and regularly utilized to evaluate performance. In most cases, I think a three-year Strategic Plan is a useful timeline, although I've been on company boards that can effectively plan for five years and beyond, complete with excellent financial modeling. Much depends on a time horizon that is predictable and appropriate for your type of business.

While one can quibble on how long a Strategic Plan needs to be, your Annual Plan is a "must," and by that, I mean your Annual Plan should be reviewed every three to six months. Don't let a few months slip by because you're caught up in the "tyranny of the urgent" or feel that since the company seems to be sailing along you don't need to trim the sails or review where you're going.

You always want to know exactly where you are, if for no other reason than if you are off by a degree or two, you could miss your target by a mile if enough time passes.

Look at your Annual Plan as an excellent management tool to assess how your current year is performing versus your plans and expectations. If you have a middle management team, including them in your Annual Plan is an excellent way to get them involved in "owning" the upcoming year's plan. Over time they will learn to become better planners.

When budgeting, it's helpful to have broad guidance from your board of directors (if you have one) or from mentors who are conversant about growth rates, financial expectations, and outstanding receivables, etc. I like to encourage bottom-up budgeting, which means involving the persons responsible for delivering the results. Once the overall plan is accepted, the Annual Plan should be broken down into the twelve months so that you can evaluate month-by-month whether or not you are meeting your targets.

If you're on target, great. If you're not, what's off? Could revenue be slower than projected? Are expenses higher than expected? Or a combination of both?

Discuss if you can or if you should take corrective action at this point. Focus on what action is necessary to get back on plan— and be realistic about what is achievable. When things start to deviate from your plan, corrective action sooner rather than later is always better than waiting too long to take the right corrective action.

We saw this happen at SuperNet. Not long after we launched our business, we began offering to design websites for our customers. Not only that, but we advertised that we would "customize your website to fit your specific business."

That all sounded great—on paper. Customers loved hearing that we would custom-design a website for them at a reasonable price. As I recall, minimal websites were $250 while more complex ones with all the bells and whistles could cost up to $4,000.

We noticed, however, that we weren't making any money in our web design department even though we were quite busy and had hired excellent web designers who received glowing reports from satisfied customers. Our problem was that we were starting design from scratch with every last customer. Thus we were not very efficient with our labor.

Here's what we did to fix that. First, we studied the websites we were building and realized that a lot of them were fairly similar. One of our designers suggested that if we could develop three or four templates for a website—the "guts"—then we could use one of those templates as the foundation for any website. A template website could still be "tweaked," meaning the customer would still be receiving a customized solution to the building of his website.

We also explained to our web design people how important it was to listen closely to customers on what they were looking for in a website. Once our design team received that input, they could present the best template and explain why this type of website would best match the marketing and information needs of a particular business.

Going through this exercise helped us to see that we needed to be upfront with the customer about what we could and could not do in terms of website design. If customers wanted additional work, then we needed to properly quantify the additional cost and adjust the contract. Customization was a good thing for our business, but we didn't realize how much additional costs we were absorbing until we looked at the expenses we were tracking as part of our Annual Plan review.

When these two changes were put into place, our web design department became profitable.

Developing systems that enhance efficiency have greater and faster payback for large-scale companies. That doesn't mean I'm a fan of detailed hundred-page documents just because it looks more thorough: more often than not, less is more in these cases.

A concise documentation of key operating procedures, for instance, builds consistency and serves as a valuable reference for any employee moving into a new responsibility. You'll also find that a tight, concise document will help your company meet federal and state regulations.

There's no reason to re-invent the wheel when it comes to Annual Plans and Strategic Plans. Consider using past plans as templates, editing them to match what you're doing. Templates can jump-start planning activity and enhance productivity, like when lending organizations employ template "forms" for mortgage applications, which enables bankers to quickly analyze the data and make a decision on the loan worthiness of the applicant.

Last but not least, given today's rapidly changing electronic channels, give a high priority to your website and social media feedback.

Performance Planning and Monitoring

You'll never go wrong as an entrepreneur if you decide to make performance planning and performance monitoring "good practices" for your upstart company.

Performance planning should be linked to the key strategic objectives and the specific things in a person's "influence domain," which contributes to that objective. The key performance measures should have major impact on company performance. Rather than a performance plan that has a list of attributes subject to objective judgment, I like to see key items that do three things:
- tie into the annual plan
- have impact in delivering that plan
- can be measured

Many companies today develop these five-to-seven KPMs, or Key Performance Measurements. These KPMs can be monitored daily, weekly, or monthly. When you can identify both financial and non-financial measurements, then you can compile these into a balanced "scorecard."

Here's a real-life example:

At my Hampton Inn, there are four key performance measurements that I regularly review with my managers:

- occupancy rate
- average daily rate, or ADR, which refers to the average rate we were able to receive for all the rooms that night
- customer satisfaction
- employee satisfaction

The occupancy and ADR are known daily and can be readily reviewed against monthly goals. Customer satisfaction is monitored monthly by Hilton's surveys that are emailed to customers, which is greatly beneficial to us because we can see how we compare to 800 other Hampton Inns and Suites in the Hilton system; and employee satisfaction can be measured by attendance and an annual survey. All four are specific and measurable. If these four are on track, we know we're performing well at the Hampton Inn.

I've worked with corporate and not-for-profit boards to develop KPMs to help them measure their progress against major key strategic initiatives or major goals identified in their Annual Plan. I will share two examples that I helped develop—one for an insurance company and one for a university.

In the first example with an insurance company in which I served as a treasurer, the team and I identified six major KPMs to monitor:

1. Financial stability
2. Profitability
3. Quality products
4. Mix of business
5. Productivity
6. Relationship and service

Each performance "indicator" has anywhere from two-to-four specific things that get measured quarterly—a test of where we are in relation to the primary goals and also in relation to historical achievements.

Now take a look at my second example, which comes from the world of academia. For this particular university, we identified five key performance indicators, or KPIs:

1. Student body
2. Admissions
3. Financial aid
4. Staff and faculty
5. Operational stability

These types of evaluations are invaluable to members of the board of directors because they can see—at a glance—what is going well, what isn't, and what the issues are. Boards usually have limited time to quickly get a broad overview of where things stand.

I see several advantages to producing a chart like this, which can help the board and the staff agree on what is critical to be worked on. Accountability is enhanced greatly because the board and staff are working out how performance will be measured in a way that everyone clearly understands what is expected.

What I love about key performance indicators is how the measurements are black and white and their importance can be understood by every employee. Along those lines, one of the most effective communication tools—and a motivator as well—is the use of "visual management." By this I mean an easily understood and highly visual feedback from a poster, for example. Even in the day of computers and mobile devices, I find that a simple colorful chart that measures an important aspect of our business to be quite useful for all employees.

At our Hampton Inn, we have a large poster inside the office behind the front desk that lists the occupancy rates and ADR goal for the month printed at the top of the poster. Each day's results are entered for these two goals—green if we hit or exceed the goal, and red if we did not make the goal.

My general managers and assistant general managers are especially keen to see the results because they know they will receive a bonus if they surpass certain goals for the occupancy rate and the average daily rate. That's why, when I've walked into that office, taken a long look, and said, "I like green!", my upper management team laughs. They know these key performance measurements are tied to the extra green they hope to receive.

The lesson to be learned about launching a business is this: While each new business has different needs and different measurements, the waters are calmed with good planning. Implementation of these systems will enhance productivity, align performance planning and monitoring, and provide constant feedback.

FIVE

Thinking Morally, Acting Ethically

"The argument in defense of free enterprise trades heavily on the maturity, intelligence, and responsibility of those operating within the economic system."

—Richard De George, author of *Business Ethics*

"Pretending you're moral, saying you're moral, is not the same as acting morally."

—Alan Dershowitz, American lawyer, jurist, and author

I've harped a great deal on the importance of having a Values Statement and regularly referring to your declaration of values after you launch your business. After all, you won't want to lose sight of what you've decided is important to you and your company.

But here's another thing I'd like you to do with your Values Statement: Get in the habit of reviewing your values *before* you interview prospective new employees. That way, your principles and ethics will be foremost in your mind during the interview process—and you'll be able to articulate those values. If you decide to hire that person, your new employee will have a perfunctory understanding of the ethics that guide your business. By taking this important step, you'll be laying down foundational blocks that build a strong ethical culture in your company.

I understand that ethics often get overlooked—or forgotten completely—in many corporate environments. That's a shame because I believe that hewing to a certain set of principles promotes ethical behavior. Doing the right thing never goes out of style.

Webster's New World Dictionary describes ethics as conforming to certain moral standards or conforming to professional standards of conduct. The core values undergirding ethical thinking boil down to four things:

- Do no harm
- Promote good
- Be fair
- Look for equality

Don't expect your new employee to pick up your ethical stance from a job interview since his focus may be elsewhere during the process. The time to drill down on ethics training—at least to how it pertains to your company—is during orientation training. Most persons want to do what is right, but situations will arise when it's not always clear what the "right" decision or "wrong" decision should be in a certain situation.

Rushworth Kidder, founder of the Institute for Global Ethics and author of *How Good People Make Tough Choices: Resolving the Dilemmas of Ethical Living*, says that decision-making is driven by our core values and fall into two different categories: moral temptations and ethical dilemmas.

A moral temptation is a decision that you make based on what you perceive to be right or wrong. So what is right and what is wrong?

That's a question that's been asked since Eve was picking apples in the Garden, but you are generally thought to be in the wrong if you:

- violate the law
- depart from the truth
- deviate from moral integrity

Just because something is legal doesn't make it right. Kidder describes three tests for right versus wrong:

1. The stench test: Does making a certain decision give off an indefinable odor or a bad feeling in the pit of your stomach? This is where the term "gut check" comes into play.

2. The front-page test: If your decision is plastered all over the front page of your local newspaper, would that be a big deal to you? In other words, would you make a different decision if you knew that your decision would become public knowledge?

3. The Mom test: In other words, what would your mom do in this situation? Do you hear her words reverberating in your brain? *Young lady, a job worth doing is worth doing right.*

An ethical dilemma means you're facing a choice between two entirely different options even though both have elements of being "right." You could say that it all depends on how you look at the issue. An example could be the current political debate about coal mining: Is it right to protect the environment from dirty air or is it right to protect these all-important energy jobs that drive the local and national economy? Kidder says that when people encounter tough choices like this, they aren't facing a moral temptation but rather an ethical dilemma with two sides to consider.

Kidder suggests four different paradigms for understanding ethical dilemmas:

1. Truth vs. loyalty. This means the truth is in conformity with facts or reality. Loyalty means being allegiant to other people or the company you work for. Kidder says it's right to stand for the truth, but it's also right to be loyal.

2. Short term vs. the long term. Short-term concerns means taking care of today while preserving the possibility of the future. Long-term concerns means taking the long view and not being so concerned about the short-term impacts. Kidder says it's just as right to plan for the short term as it is for the long term.

3. The individual vs. the community. We all want to be individuals free to pursue our own interests, meaning the rights of the individual are preserved. When we talk about the community, we're saying the needs of the majority outweigh the interests of the individual. Kidder says it's okay to consider the rights of the individual as well as the community.

4. Justice vs. mercy. When you stick to your principles, you seek justice. When you seek benevolence, you show mercy for the particular needs of an individual. Kidder says it's right to be merciful and it's right to enforce justice.

When you have a very difficult decision to make, think about which category best fits your type of dilemma. Doing so can provide a helpful framework. On close calls, Kidder suggests you lean toward truth over loyalty, long term over short term, and community over the individual. As for the justice vs. mercy dilemma, I think you'll find this one to be the most difficult to apply fairly. I personally prefer to show mercy, but sometimes justice is required when certain consequences need to happen.

As they say, it all depends on the situation . . . .

Here's an example of a difficult ethical dilemma that I was involved in when I was the chairman of a local Habitat for Humanity chapter. In case you're not aware of this worthwhile ministry, Habitat for Humanity is devoted to building simple, decent, and affordable homes that are sold or rented to the less fortunate for no profit.

At our local Habitat for Humanity chapter in the Lancaster area, we had around sixty homes that we were either holding the mortgage on or renting to disadvantaged families. We hired an excellent bilingual receptionist in the office who took care of receiving the mortgage and rental payments from our home owners and renters, many of whom paid in cash. Sofia, a Hispanic single-parent mom, was excellent in the way she communicated with the Habitat house owners and renters and was highly regarded in the Latino community. We liked her as well and offered Sofia and her two children the opportunity to rent a two-bedroom apartment above our Habitat office.

One evening I received a confidential call from the chairman of our Family Selection Committee. She told me that several owners were claiming they had paid their mortgage but our records did not show payment. When the Habitat treasurer followed up, we found additional irregularities, including several checks made out by this receptionist to suppliers for whom we had no invoice.

Something was fishy. Upon further investigation, it was clear that she was embezzling funds and writing fraudulent checks—both serious matters. We caught her red-handed, but our executive committee was split on what to do. Some wanted to turn the matter over to the police and let them deal with it, while others wanted to give her a second chance.

We were clearly dealing with a situation that fit the justice vs. mercy category. As board chairman, I found the Kidder model to be incredibly helpful as we struggled about what to do with Sofia, who was a single mother, a good worker, an excellent communicator, and well respected and even loved by the families we served through Habitat for Humanity.

The problem was that Sofia was also dishonest and not trustworthy. The board was split down the middle, with some Habitat board members feeling that the severity of the matter called for immediate dismissal and turning over the evidence to the police for prosecution. "Justice must be served," they said.

The other half favored mercy, wanting to give her a second chance and not ruin her life. "Show mercy as you would want to be shown mercy," they said.

In the end, we compromised. We dismissed her from her job with Habitat for Humanity and asked her and her family to move out of their apartment. But we also told her that we would not be reporting the theft of monies to the police, which could have meant possible jail time and leaving her children as foster children. We supported her with counseling, allowed her two months of free rent, and helped her find a new apartment.

I felt good about the outcome. We had been gracious and as helpful as possible to an employee who had made a terrible choice. While some board members were concerned that we had been too lenient, it seemed the right decision. We had "leaned" toward mercy, and I didn't think that was a bad thing.

My kumbaya feelings were challenged two years later, however, when I received a confidential call from another organization asking if Sofia had worked for us and if we had ever had an embezzling problem with her.

My heart sank. She had not learned from the mercy we showed her and actually had done the opposite—she had stolen money from her new employer, and in this situation, she needed the full force of the law to be thrown at her.

All this goes to show that justice vs. mercy situations are not easy.

Arriving at Decisions

Since your Values Statement is the building block for your corporate culture, using employee orientation and other training venues to promote and reinforce those values will keep your new company on a straight track. There will likely be numerous occasions when you and your management team could have made a better decision or carried out a difficult enforcement, but at least your team will understand how you arrived at those decisions because they were defined by your values.

A perfect illustration of this happened about six months after we launched SuperNet. This would have been sometime in 1994.

One afternoon, one of our technicians—a young twenty-two-year-old fresh out of college—approached Rod.

"Are you aware of the porn site that we are transmitting as part of our Internet services?" he asked.

Rod's ears perked up after hearing that statement. "No, I haven't," he said. "What's happening."

"Well, it's like this," the technician said. He explained that one of our best business accounts had launched a website that showed sexually explicit photos of naked women—for a fee, naturally.

Remember, this was the early days of the Internet, when purveyors of porn were discovering that there was a huge market for this type of fare. No longer did men have to shop for skin magazines in convenience stores or drive to a seedy part of town to watch an X-rated movie. Everything they wanted to see was a few clicks away in the privacy of their home.

Our young employee remembered from his employee orientation that Rod and I had declared that one of our core values was "treating all persons with dignity." He didn't think what was on that porn site was treating persons, especially women, with dignity, and we wholeheartedly agreed with that assessment.

Rod, Carlton, and I looked at the porn site—very quickly, I might add—and immediately knew it was very bad!

So, what should we do? The person behind the site was one of our bigger customers with a number of businesses. Fortunately, as part of our culture, we had a clause in our "Business Services Internet Agreement" that spoke to our values. Clause No. 18 stated that SuperNet's desire was "to transmit wholesome content."

The three of us decided to invoke that clause as the reason we could no longer transmit such material. When we informed our client that he would need to discontinue the porn site, he took umbrage. "You cannot make me do that!" he bellowed. "There's the First Amendment, you know. Besides, I've put a lot of money into this site, so I have to protect my investment. I'm not taking it down!"

Nonetheless, we decided to hold to our position and gave him three days to discontinue the porn site, or we would need to discontinue his service.

Day 1: still on.

Day 2: still on.

By now, we had forty-six employees at SuperNet, and our standoff at the O.K. Corral had circulated through the company. Would we stick to our guns?

Day 3: still on.

He wasn't going to back down. We called him to give him a final chance to remove the porn site.

"No way," he replied. "Shut me down, and I'll sue you so quickly that it will make your head spin."

The prospect of hiring an attorney and incurring significant legal bills gave us pause—for just a few minutes. We weren't going to back down either.

"We're taking your site down tomorrow," we said.

After we cut him off the next day, the guy took his porn site elsewhere and didn't take us to court. (He probably didn't want to run up legal bills either.)

And what happened to SuperNet? We feel vindicated because since that standoff, we grew from forty-six employees to over 1,500 employees—and firmly believe the stand we took as a company was a bulwark for upholding our values.

I want to impress upon you how clearly communicating corporate responsibility—to your employees, your vendors, your community, and to the world—needs to be part of your corporate culture. This aspect of "social entrepreneurship" is encouraging firms to think about adopting a B Corporation classification.

B Corporations are a recent form of legal organization where a for-profit firm, in addition to reporting its financial results, also commits to measuring its positive impact on its work force, the community, and the environment. Transparency and accountability are hallmarks of B Corps. The B Corp structure is something I'd strongly recommend you look into as you determine your best legal structure, especially if your idea is focused on a social cause.

I'm very encouraged by the growing interest in "social entrepreneurship," especially by today's Millennials. Social entrepreneurship is a way to bring a community together—under a business endeavor—to find practical solutions to problems we face today as a society. In other words, the primary goal is to meet a social need, not just make a profit.

We have two excellent examples in my hometown of Lancaster. The first is a B Corporation company started by a woman entrepreneur called The Stroopie Co. (Visit www.stroopies.com.) This company makes Dutch stroopwafels—rich, flavorful cinnamon-and-caramel cookie snacks—that are quite tasty with your morning coffee. They've hired refugees to make the stroopwafels as way to support them and their families who are starting over in Lancaster after fleeing their war-torn countries. The Stroopie

Co. submits the firm to B Corporate scoring of their social impact, and they currently hold an 83 rating.

The second example is the Lancaster Food Company (visit www.thelancasterfoodcompany.com), which makes certified organic breads and organic maple syrup. Their company goal is to "provide a fair wage for persons with background issues that make getting a job difficult." In addition to offering a hand up rather than a handout, the management team incorporates emotional support as an important part of their employment activity. They are making a positive impact in Lancaster by their focus on hiring people out of poverty.

Both of these businesses, and others like them, are driven by "a cause," although they also need to carefully manage the business by the principles promoted in this book, such as managing cash flow, etc., to remain sustainable. Nonetheless, I applaud these entrepreneurs for their dedication to the social aspect of their entrepreneurial endeavors, and the positive impact they are making across America and the world.

It's all about what you value as a company, right? Whatever you do, I want you to think creatively about how you can help your employees buy into your corporate values statement. When I was a senior vice president at High Industries in Lancaster, our leadership team worked at revising what we thought would be a good values statement for all of our existing companies and for our planned expansions into other businesses.

We sent the draft out to our 2,000 employees, asking for their input and feedback. We received over 200 responses, which led us to making several important improvements to our Values Statement. Equally important, the employees had ownership of the process.

When I subsequently formed new businesses for this family holding company, I utilized our revised values statement with all the employees, from the president to the front-line persons.

And that's when you know that you're all pulling from the same rope.

Work and Family

Let's consider the word *balance*. Friends who know me best understand that this is one of my favorite words.

Launching a business can be all-consuming and gobble up many hours of the day. Sure, you'll have to persevere and perhaps put in twelve-hour days at the beginning, but let me remind you that family and relationships are more important than any business launch. This is why I urge you to pay attention to the needs of your dear family and friends.

When I was a young executive, rapidly climbing the corporate ladder, I found it hard to say no to "opportunities" that I thought would enhance my job performance. If I was invited to breakfast or dinner meetings by my boss or vendors, I said yes because I thought these business-related encounters would earn me brownie points, increase my networking circle, and boost my personal development.

At the time, though, I was the father of three young children, and even though I thought I was doing a good job making time for them, I had the habit of moving family plans around when a business need arose. I naturally assumed that my family could adjust to schedule changes easier than business clients, who had travel commitments and busy schedules fixed in advance.

Late one afternoon, I called home and informed Doris that I wouldn't be home for dinner because I had a "late change" in my schedule because the only time a business client could see me was after 6 p.m. Of course, this was on top of all the evenings I was gone because of another "important" meeting or report to finish.

When I got home that evening, my dear and normally supportive wife put her foot down: "If you can find time to schedule meetings every night for business, you certainly can do the same for the family. What night of the week can we schedule you for?"

There was an edge to her voice. I wasn't used to that tone coming from my dear wife, so I knew she was serious.

I backpedaled. "Okay, let's see what we can do," I said. She had a point—maybe I did need to *schedule* my family for an evening from Monday through Friday.

I pulled out my DayTimer. (This was back in the days before cell phones or tablet computers.) I looked over my upcoming evening commitments. Most Friday nights were open, so I said, "Okay, Friday night looks best."

"Super. Friday night it is. Friday night is Family Night. Put it in your book."

From then on, I blocked out Friday evenings and started a "Friday Family Night" tradition, which turned out to be one of the best things I ever did during my corporate career. I wanted our kids to be invested in well, so Mom and I told them that they could take turns picking what we would do together as a family.

We allowed their imagination to soar. What variety! Our youngest son, Jeff, said he wanted to go to a Friday night flea market called the Green Dragon. He didn't want to walk the aisles looking at stuff—he wanted to go there because he liked getting cotton candy.

Rod voted to go bowling on Friday nights, so we did that even though Debbie couldn't bowl very well when she was young. She asked to go rafting in the summer, and in the winter, she asked if we could go night skiing at Roundtop Mountain Resort, a ski hill about forty-five minutes west of Lancaster.

Looking back, I'm grateful for the time I spent with my family during those critical years, and for those memories—thank you, Honey! The children are now adults, raising their own families, and I almost missed out on a once-in-a-lifetime chance to be an involved father. I know myself . . . without Doris's demanding push, I bet I would have booked half of those Friday nights for business.

Another behavior to begin practicing is giving back in some form. Giving of your time, your talents, and your money is rewarding and sets an excellent example for your employees. You can encourage everyone signing up for a "service day" in the community—but make sure your name is on the top of the list. Otherwise, employee morale will sink fast.

I salute entrepreneurs who support a worthy cause in their communities. That support should be tangible. By that I mean you must lead by example, which is often done by writing a check. You don't have to tell your employees how much, but they need to see you giving.

I love entrepreneurs who think in this fashion. One of the emerging entrepreneurs who hired me as a consultant decided from day one that every year in December he would hold a meeting with his employees to let them help decide how the company would distribute a certain percentage of its net income.

A few years later, when his fledgling company had grown to twelve employees, the December exercise was a unifying and rewarding activity for the entire team. Giving became cemented as part of this company's culture. What a way to integrate a value!

Bad Apples

Discussing corporate values and giving to others are the noble side of starting a business. Now let's pivot to something not as pleasant: What can you do if there has been unacceptable behavior within your organization?

My advice is to always deal with the situation openly and quickly, and as honestly as possible. If possible, use the situation as a learning opportunity. Avoid knee-jerk reactions, which are totally normal in situations like this. A learning organization (and for that matter, a learning individual) allows for mistakes but corrects them and learns from them. Depending on the severity of the situation, you may need to take disciplinary action to reinforce the seriousness of the undesirable behavior.

When I was in the senior leadership at High Industries, one of the companies that I oversaw held a Christmas party. Again, companies under the High Industries umbrella had a lot of autonomy, which means the employees took the lead in planning the Christmas party.

When I stepped into the employee lunchroom on an afternoon in December, there was a lot of laughter and holiday good cheer. I believe the punch was spiked. (Again, this was more than twenty-five years ago, when things were different regarding alcohol in the workplace.)

Everyone was having a nice time when suddenly a rollicking Santa entered through the lunchroom door with a boom box in his hand. He was dancing up a storm.

"Ho, ho, ho!" he bellowed. "Merry Christmas everyone, especially those who have been naughty in the last year."

People laughed, and I thought this fake Santa was just trying to be funny. Santa put the boom box on the floor and pressed a button. A rock 'n' roll version of *Jingle Bells* played, which was all he needed to dance to the music.

All in good fun, right?

When Jingle Bells was over, the music suddenly shifted to a boom-boom beat—and Santa changed from a "good Santa" to a "bad Santa." First, he whipped off his black boots and flung them toward a couple of women, which prompted a few laughs. Then he unbuckled his red pants and flung them away—followed by his thick black belt and brilliant red coat trimmed with white faux fur. The fake beard and tall hat stayed on, however, which left Santa wearing nothing more than a smile and a red Speedo.

"Ho, ho, ho!" he bellowed again. "Who would like some holiday cheer?"

Several women raised their hands. As the big beat song continued to play, he sidled up a welcoming woman and gyrated his pelvis like Elvis used to do, which prompted more laughter from the ladies. I think they call it "grinding."

I wasn't laughing. Neither was every woman. Several were visibly upset. The party was spinning out of control. *Oh, boy. If Dale High saw this . . . .*

I was wondering what to do when Santa wrapped up his shtick, gathered his clothes, and departed with a hearty "Ho, ho, ho."

I looked around the room for the company president. When I made eye contact, I motioned for him to meet me in the back of the lunchroom.

"Well," I said. "What happened?"

The president was embarrassed—but he didn't look too concerned.

"I know what you're thinking, Allon," he said. "I delegated the party planning to the packaging department. Obviously, this randy Santa was their idea. I'm just as surprised as you are."

"I think we're going to have some trouble," I commented.

"Really?"

"You'll see."

The next day, I received a phone call from one of the packaging employees. She told me she was upset about the stripping

Santa act and demanded to meet with me and the company president.

"No problem," I said.

The following day, in the same conference room, she faced me and the company and unloaded a broadside—respectfully, I might add.

"I know this company values respect for all persons, and that show wasn't appropriate at all. I thought Santa was suggestive, lewd, and totally out of character for this company," she said. "This was totally over the top. I think this could have been sexual harassment."

Hearing the words *sexual harassment* set off alarm bells. That could mean a lawyer would be involved, followed by a claim and an out-of-court settlement for probably tens of thousands of dollars. That's the last thing anyone wanted. The company president and I looked at each other. We needed to nip this in the bud.

"Ma'am, on behalf of High Industries, I apologize for what happened. I can assure you that we will take steps to make sure something like this doesn't happen again."

My next move was for us to meet with the planning committee for the company Christmas party. We shared how the stripping Santa had upset several employees and how his lewd performance was not consistent with our values. The planning chairman was a female, so when I asked her why she and her team thought it would be a good idea to book a "naughty Santa," she replied that she thought it would be a fun way to spark up a dull Christmas party. After hearing our concerns, however, she and the committee agreed that his "show" was inappropriate and wouldn't happen again.

Normally, that would be the end of the matter, but since one of our female employees had mentioned the phrase "sexual harassment," I felt that we needed to meet with her to share what steps we had taken to address her concerns. We took our time describing our follow-up meeting with the event planners and how everyone agreed that "bad Santa" never should have happened. She was gracious and thanked us for our concern—and decided to let the matter drop.

So here's the bottom line: no one got fired, no one got sued, and we were able to use the matter as reinforcement of our values and desired culture.

A different type of "bad behavior" happened when I received a phone call from my internal accounting person at our Weaver Inc. headquarters. The woman on the line told me she was concerned that our cash sales of over-the-counter eggs sales from an egg-raising operation we owned in North Carolina had dipped quite a bit below normal.

At the time, I was chairman of the company's board of directors, so I had oversight responsibilities. I thought we had an excellent relationship with the on-site manager who reported to me. I'll call him Carl.

When I called him to inquire why the eggs sales had dropped, Carl said, "Well, we have an unusual situation that I was just quietly taking care of, and I thought it might be better if I just kept it away from you."

It might be better to keep it away from you.

No one in a position of authority or leadership wants to hear that. My feelings were bruised as well because I thought Carl and I had an open, honest, transparent relationship and enjoyed working together.

"Okay, tell me what's happening," I said.

It seemed that an international team of agriculture major students—mainly from the Philippines—had spent a few days visiting our operation to see how this particular business was done in the

U.S. One of the students had "fallen in love" with the daughter of one of our employees.

When the team was set to return to Asia, this young man skipped his flight and somehow found his way back to our company. Now what do you do with this modern-day Romeo and Juliet?

My manager and her family came up with plan to help hide him until he could marry this gal, which would mean he could remain in the U.S. Until that happened, my manager had put him to work painting and doing odd jobs, paying him out of the "egg cash" drawer. He also provided him a place to live in an abandoned building on our premise.

Like I always say, just when you think you've heard it all . . .

I had multiple reactions. First, my trust in my manager came into question. I was disappointed he had chosen not to discuss this with me. Second, using company cash and a company-owned building to help hide an illegal alien was totally out of the question for our company. We had over 400 immigrants working for us, and we were always above board and sensitive to making sure they were in this country legally.

I knew we could not risk having him taken away by the U.S. Immigration and Custom Enforcement (ICE), which would open up a whole different can of worms, so we had a justice vs. mercy dilemma on our hands.

Then my manager told me all the employees who knew about the situation agreed with his decision, and if I ordered it stopped, they would all view it as a big corporation pushing the little guy and promoting "Yankee insensitivity."

There were some serious headwinds, but I felt we absolutely could not be a party to hiding an illegal alien in our facility and paying him under the table until he married this American girl.

"If you want to support the young man, you'll have to find another way," I said. "Corporately, we cannot be involved."

The lesson to be learned here is this: Culture is driven by the values you emphasize. Once you launch your company, you can be sure that you'll sail into choppy ethical waters.

Know how you're going to steer the boat before you get there!

SIX

Navigating the Rough Seas

"I've never known a man worth his salt who in the long run, deep down in his heart, didn't appreciate the grind, and the discipline. I firmly believe that any man's finest hour—this great fulfillment to all he holds dear—is that moment when he has worked his heart out in a good cause and lies exhausted on the field of battle victorious."

—Vince Lombardi, legendary NFL coach

"Most of the important things in the world have been accomplished by people who have kept on trying when there seemed to be no hope at all."

—Dale Carnegie, American writer and lecturer on self-improvement, salesmanship, and interpersonal skills

Have you ever been on the water when the seas suddenly turned turbulent with wind, waves, and storms?

I've never been a sailor per se, so I can't say that I've personally experienced being in a vessel when a small craft advisory was issued by the National Weather Service. But I have looked out from our cottage on the Chesapeake Bay when there's been a gale force warning and witnessed huge whitecaps covering the bay and boats bobbing like apples. *I'm sure glad I'm not out there on the water*, I've thought.

I did get caught once in a small boat on a lake in North Carolina when a thunderstorm suddenly hit. Not fun!

Or think of a typical Royal Caribbean cruise ship. With so many souls on board—5,000 passengers and another 2,500 crew members—I can only imagine the huge responsibility that a ship captain bears on his shoulders. I'm sure he's well aware of the captains who made huge mistakes that cost them their ships, their lives, and their passengers' lives.

Well, I shouldn't say mistakes. I should say they got into trouble because of *complacency*.

The most famous example is Captain Edward Smith of the *RMS Titanic*, which struck an iceberg on April 15, 1912 at 2:20 a.m., punching several holes in the hull. The English captain, in his final voyage at the helm of a ship, was shooting to set a record for an Atlantic crossing; hence his decision not to slow the gigantic passenger ship even though there were reports of icebergs in the vicinity. Captain Smith didn't heed the warnings because he believed the ship was unsinkable. In fact, Captain Smith originally failed to call for an evacuation because he thought the leak could be contained.

Complacency led to his decision not to have enough lifeboats on board, and the subsequent lack of training created an unbelievable amount of chaos after the ship struck the iceberg. The lifeboats were boarded haphazardly, and many left the ship half-full because the crew were ill-prepared to deal with an emergency disembarking. A total of 1,517 people lost their lives in the frigid waters that night.

Nearly one hundred years later, in our lifetimes, the *Costa Concordia* ran aground off the Italian coast because Captain Francesco Schettino became complacent when he navigated the cruise ship too close to the Isola del Giglio. The reason? He wanted to show his wealthy passengers a better view of the Tuscan village.

Like the captain of the *Titanic*, the *Costa Concordia* captain failed to realize the magnitude of his mistake—or believe that he had really messed up. In the chaos, he failed to evacuate passengers quickly—and he was one of the first to abandon ship. Thirty-two people died who could have survived, and Captain Schettino was sentenced to sixteen years in prison.

You have to expect the unexpected when you launch your business. Your mindset shouldn't be *I can sink at any time* but this: *There's always a storm brewing.* Monitoring your expenses and sales closely will mentally prepare you for any turbulence that's to come. Keeping a close tab on your employees' job performance—without falling into the micro-managing pit—should allow you to spot where you're short and where you're overstocked with labor. (The cost of employees is often your biggest budget line item.)

So, having a good Annual Plan, a good operating system in place, and good monitoring can help guide the firm through the turbulent times that are sure to arrive.

This is a good place to reiterate the importance of planning. The initial plan is the Business Plan, followed by a Strategic Plan with a three-to-five-year outlook, and then you can map out an Annual Plan. Plans are like maps; they remind you of the direction you need to take your new company. You want to refer to them time and again.

Once you and your management team are all on board with your Annual Plan, you should break it down into the twelve months of the year so that you can monitor your business month-by-month and evaluate if your firm is functioning as expected.

For example, at the Hampton Inn, I mentioned that I have four key measurements that I review with managers on a regular basis. They are:

1. occupancy rate versus our plan

2. average daily rate, meaning the money we received divided by the number of rooms we rented that night, versus our plan

3. customer satisfaction versus our plan

4. employee satisfaction versus our plan

Those are the keystones. But I have three other key performance measurements that I keep a close tab on. They are:

5. total revenue versus our plan

6. total expenses versus our plan

7. net income versus our plan

I encourage you to develop anywhere from five-to-seven key measurements that will tell you if you're performing to plan, just as I have outlined here.

You'll notice that the last three are financial measurements—or what most people call "the bottom line." I review these numbers with my managers, but you'll have to determine how comfortable you are sharing this amount of financial information. I can assure you that the more financial information you share, the more your employees in upper management will understand about your business. Perhaps they will spot something that you're overlooking.

The reason I strongly recommend monthly monitoring is that the sooner you observe a deviation from the plan, the sooner you can take advantage of better-than-expected performance—or make the necessary adjustments to get back on track if corrective action is needed.

This monthly monitoring is an activity that provides you an excellent opportunity to develop your people, to involve them in appropriate modifications to the plan if required, and to communicate factually about performance.

A good culture will develop both the heart and mind of your employees. This monthly activity between you and your key employees, done right, will build a trusted relationship and almost always result in better outcomes as you work together, focused on performance.

Meet Chet

I met Chester A. Raber years ago when we were both working for High Industries in Lancaster. Don't let the 19th-century first name fool you: everyone calls him "Chet."

Chet's job at High Industries was to train our management teams how to become participative managers. Sounds easy on paper, but it wasn't.

Chet says today's work force mirrors the culture at large, meaning that employees want to have more say in what happens on the shop floor. Employees want to work in an environment where they are respected by their supervisors for being "producers," and they want to be supported as well as challenged to do a good job.

What rank-and-file employees *don't* want is a rigid, my-way-or-the-highway boss who doesn't give a flip about their lives or working conditions.

"Most individuals, since the Enlightenment or even the Reformation, have been looking to be freed of the authoritarian leader," Chet said. It's his belief that when employees feel like they're playing a participatory role, they take stronger ownership and even experience a sense of joy and excitement when they come to work each day. Under those circumstances, a business is more likely to be successful and profitable.

While at High Industries, Chet developed a system that he calls the Core4 Management System, which he wrote about in his book, *The Closed Door Policy: Vitalizing People Management for the Twenty-First Century, Core4.* His main argument is that technology is changing the way we do business every day—and nothing can be done about that—but when people have their needs met in the workplace, they can assist the company in achieving the very best results.

His approach is to have bosses or managers sit down for a closed-door, one-on-one meeting, away from distractions, so that they can focus on Core4's four basic practices:

1. Working on a plan agreement
2. Building a trusting relationship
3. Striving for teamwork
4. Streamlining the decision process

Dale High at High Industries was totally on board with this management approach, and he proved to be an excellent boss and mentor. At one time, I had six companies for which I was responsible, but using the five-to-seven key performance measurements streamlined the review process for the both of us. In addition, we had an agreed-upon annual plan for each company that I would update monthly.

Our monthly one-on-one meeting was an efficient review of each company's KPMs; some would be ahead of the annual plan and others would be behind. He would compliment me on the areas where we were ahead of plan and discuss the factors impacting areas where we were below expectations. If we remained behind plan for a couple of months, we would together evaluate whether we could get back on plan or whether the plan wasn't realistic in the first place.

Dale and I would discuss any new corrective tactics that would help us get back on plan and when it might make sense to implement them. When we were nearing the end of our meeting, I'd ask Dale to review several minor things that I didn't want to bring up at our monthly meeting with other vice presidents. I thought this was the most efficient way to use his time wisely.

Dale led a successful family holding company that had twelve subsidiary companies managed in this manner. He was one of the best bosses in my entire career! A lot of that was because of the person himself, but the process he put us through was key to a smooth-working relationship where we were both aligned around an Annual Plan and five-to-seven agreed-upon key measurements, including how we would monitor the business monthly and communicate those results.

This management process implied that I would take responsibility to make decisions regarding these six companies, and rarely need to involve him on problem-solving routine matters that could and should be handled by management. The additional advantage of this approach is a fairly rapid response environment, and a well understood way in which decisions will be made. For the individual entrepreneur, it is equally important that you have a clear but rapid decision-making process, making adjustments as soon as appropriate.

Sometimes things don't go right according to plan. Sometimes new information enters the picture, or an outside factor that you could not have forecasted impacts your plan, changing your outlook overnight. That can happen, so knowing when to make adjustments calls for careful judgment, calm disposition, and superb balance.

So what can you do when things don't go as planned? If the situation isn't too severe or is expected to be a short-term problem, the emphasis should be on working as efficiently as possible, saving every penny you can to get through a rough time. Or, if you have the capacity and the money on hand, you can try activities like marketing more aggressively to improve performance.

One of the most difficult and very emotional challenges of an entrepreneur or manager is making the difficult decision to implement a major cost reduction, which usually means laying off personnel. These are persons you have hired, persons who have been loyal to you. They could be close friends, fellow church members, or civic organization colleagues—good people who need their job to support their families.

If you think the bleak situation is a short-term downturn, you may wish to explore "cutback/survival options" with your employees, especially if you're still a small company. I've seen companies openly process options instead of layoffs, evaluating alternatives such as everyone going to a four-day work week or everyone taking a "temporary" 10-to-15 percent pay cut to get through a rough patch.

Sometimes a layoff is necessary. Even under these difficult decisions, try very hard to respect the dignity of each person. Communicate honestly about the need for the action. Support the person in any way you can. If you can afford some severance or helping them find another job, do so. But it will not be easy.

Probably the most difficult day of my career was the day that— as a senior manager—I had to release sixteen employees due to a merger. The acquiring company already had the specialists who worked for us, so there was redundancy of required skills. For a day and too much of a night, I contemplated how I could best do this unpleasant and heart-wrenching task. Every one of them were good employees and loyal to the many tasks we had tackled together over the years. In the end, I decided that meeting individually with each person would be the best way to practice one of my treasured values—"treating all persons with dignity."

I did my very best. Some of the people that I had to let go were gracious and understood the circumstances; others were confident about "moving on." A significant minority, however, reacted in disbelief. They were upset.

"So this is what I get for my loyalty and commitment to this company after fifteen years—being kicked to the curb like this!" one person exploded. "You guys have no soul."

All I could do was remain grim-faced and acknowledge his pain.

By the time I called for the sixteenth employee, word had got out that the axe was falling. It was horrible day—for those I had to lay off and for those left behind. To this day, I'm not sure if I did the right thing taking the one-on-one approach; maybe I should have done more of a mass meeting. By seeing each person individually, I was able to thank these good folks for all they had done for the company and had given to me personally. "Please know that I'm trying to respect each person's dignity the best I knew how," I said.

I've also been on a company board with about 600 employees whose good market dried up over a matter of a few months, resulting in no other choice but to do massive layoffs. I'm thinking back to Rushworth Kidder's framework of how good people have to make tough decisions when there are ethical dilemma situations that fall into the "individual vs. community" framework. Unfortunately for the good of the community (our company's survival), some individuals were impacted severely in a layoff.

Another difficult and devastating problem can arise when partners—or even key managers in a business—cannot agree on the correct strategy. Again, dealing in open discussion, respecting one another as individuals, and tackling the situation in a professional manner is better than brooding or anger or not dealing honestly with the situation.

In my consulting career, I have seen instances of disagreement that appeared hopeless, but over time, a common ground was eventually found. I have been involved in other disagreements where a buy-out of a partner or the removal of a manager was the ultimate resolution. I choose not to share those stories.

The lesson to be learned here is this: Even when the seas are storming, hold fast to your values. Treat all person with dignity and work creatively at the best solution possible.

But you will need to make the difficult call.

As an entrepreneur, you're like President Harry Truman, who kept a thirteen-inch sign sitting atop his desk in the Oval Office. Etched on the sign was a phrase referring to the notion that the U.S. president—and you, the entrepreneur—have to make the tough calls and accept the ultimate responsibility for those decisions. The sign says:

The buck stops here.

SEVEN

Calming the Ocean Blue

"It is our relation to circumstances that determines their influence over us. The same wind that carries one vessel into port may blow another off shore."
—Christian Bovee, 19th century writer from New York City

"Certain characteristics are shared by entrepreneurs, but that doesn't mean these traits account for their success."
    —Dana Strangler, vice president of research and policy at the Kauffmann Foundation

"Genius is 1 percent inspiration and 99 percent perspiration."
        —Thomas Alva Edison, America's greatest inventor

A re entrepreneurs born or are they made?
        That age-old question has always given me a run for my money. I've wondered if entrepreneurs are a special breed, born into this world with a drive to succeed and take big-time risks, but that sort of thinking has always sounded pretentious to me. But are entrepreneurs created through the right education, on-the-job experience, and professional mentorship? Is that enough?

I'm not sure of the answer, but my gut tells me this: there is something special and unique about entrepreneurs. They have incredible gifts of vision, an off-the-chart ability to lead, and supreme confidence their idea will work. They have an uncommon willingness to put everything on the line to see things through.

James V. Koch is president emeritus at Old Dominion University in Norfolk, Virginia, and co-author of the 2008 book, *Born, Not Made: The Entrepreneurial Personality.* As you would expect from the book title, Koch argues that many entrepreneurs are wired that way, giving them a leg up on the ladder to success. He says that scientific literature suggests that heredity has a good deal to do with personality and behavior. "I'm not sure you can teach somebody to love to take risks," he told *Entrepreneur* magazine. "It seems hard-wired in the individual."

I nod my head—for reasons I'll explain shortly—but as a college professor who's taught budding entrepreneurs in the latter part of my life, I believe entrepreneurship can also be taught. I know that I've inspired others to go for it—to be passionate about their entrepreneurship idea, which is why I'm writing this book. I've have consulted with dozens of entrepreneurs over the years and walked them through the business launch and beyond. I've held hands along the way and given encouraging pats on the back.

I've worked with people who weren't natural risk-takers, but once they studied the market, did their necessary research, and considered the unpredictability of going into business on their own, they were confident they could move ahead because they understand the risk/reward percentage behind their venture.

At the end of the day, though, I will say that there is something to the heredity side—that entrepreneurs are born that way. I say that because of the family I grew up in, which I think you'll find interesting.

My great-uncle traveled to France a few years back to research our ancestry. What he was able to discover was our lineage going back fifteen generations to the 17th century when my fifteenth great-grandfather was a French nobleman with a coat of arms for the Lefever name. He lived in the eastern French region of Alsace-Lorraine, an area in the Rhine Valley that has bounced back and forth from French and German control for centuries.

Back in the late 1600s, my ancestors in Alsace-Lorraine were part of a breakaway from the Roman Catholic Church that started during the Reformation when Martin Luther nailed his *Ninety-Five Thesis* on a German church door in 1517. More than 150 years later, my Protestant family became Mennonites, the name of a new movement sweeping the land. Mennonites were followers of Menno Simon, a former Catholic priest from Friesland (a region known today as the Netherlands), who started the Christian denomination. Mennonites were a "peace church," much like the Quakers, who believed there were too many swords, too much violence, and too much killing in the world.

The Catholics looked at Mennonites as heretics because they didn't believe in infant baptism but practiced "re-baptism," meaning that they believed youngsters should wait until they were the age of majority (usually around age twelve) before they could decide whether they wanted to follow Christ. If they said, yes, they could be baptized and proclaim their faith in God. This explains why the Mennonites were also called Anabaptists. They pointed to Mark 16:16 (NIV), which says "Whoever believes and is baptized will be saved"—meaning you believe first and then you're baptized.

The Catholics, as I mentioned, looked at that type of practice as being heretical. In those days, they burned heretics at the stake or killed them with their swords.

A vigilante party swarmed the farm of my 14th great-grandfather in the Alsace-Lorraine region. The Catholic attackers surrounded the farmhouse. Inside were my 14th great-grandparents and their five children, frightened to death.

CHART SHOWING EIGHT GENERATIONS OF LEFEVERES COVERING A PERIOD OF TWO HUNDRED AND SIXTY YEARS

Mengen 1510
John 1540
Philip 1574
Andrew 1604

Abraham 1632 — Andrew 1636 — Simon 1640 — Judith 1644 imprisoned — Isacc 1648 martyred

Judith 1660 martyred — Philip 1664 martyred — Jacob 1666 martyrd — Isaac 1669 escaped — Mary 1671 martyred — Susanna 1672 martyred — Charles 1680 martyred

Abraham 1706 (A.) — Philip 1710 (P.) — Daniel 1713 (D.) — Mary 1715 — Esther 1717 — Samuel 1719 (S.)

John 1730
Peter (1733)

Isaac 1732
Catherine 1734
George 1739
Elizabeth 1742
Adam 1745
Esther 1747
Eve 1748
Jacob 1753

Christian 1737
Mary 1738
Catherine 1740
Elias 1743
David 1745
Esther 1748
Solomon 1750
Daniel 1752

Catherine 1753
Elizabeth 1755
Samuel 1757
Joseph 1760
Sarah 1763
Andrew 1767
Lydia 1770
Mary 1773

They were all murdered for their religious beliefs—except for one of the children. Isaac Lefever, fourteen years or so at the time, managed to slip out the back of the house. He hid in the barn and wasn't found after a long search.

Running for his life, Isaac traveled northward. He convinced a French silk merchant and his family to take him in somewhere along the Rhine Valley. Isaac must have been quite a preacher because he also converted them to become Anabaptists, which means *all* of them were endangered and could become martyrs during this civil war. I'm fuzzy on the details here, but the mother and the children, including Isaac, were able to flee to England because they had money and a connection to Queen Elizabeth I. I'm not sure what happened to the father; he either died or was likely killed.

The family received permission to sail to America in 1706. This was at a time when an Atlantic crossing by ship was a long, arduous, and dangerous journey that usually took three months. Crammed into a small wooden ship, rocking and rolling at the mercy of the sea, the men, women, and children endured terrible misery, stench, fumes, many kinds of seasickness, fevers, dysentery, boils, scurvy, and mouth rot from eating old and sharply salted food and meat and drinking foul water. I'm told that a third of the passengers died on these brutal trans-Atlantic trips.

The family survived and landed in New York City and eventually settled in the fertile Paradise Region of Pennsylvania, receiving a big tract of land from William Penn—the founder of the Province of Pennsylvania and an early Quaker himself.

Let's step back and think about what happened here. How entrepreneurial-minded do you have to be to step aboard a dinky wooden ship and set sail for the great unknown in frigid temperatures and gale-force winds? I'd say a lot. Risking your life to reach the New World was as entrepreneurial as you could get.

Sure, they were fleeing religious persecution, but they could have stayed in England. Instead, they caught the entrepreneurial spirit and settled in America, where Isaac's son was the first white child born in the Paradise Valley region of Pennsylvania. There's even a plaque marking the event on Route 30, the first turnpike in the country, on a stretch between Lancaster and Philadelphia. I've visited Isaac's gravestone in Paradise, which is halfway sunk into the ground. What a rich, rich family history.

I share this story because I really do think I have entrepreneurship in my blood. My grandfather and father were entrepreneurial-minded, as I'll share later. But learning about my ancestors' history was an eye-opener to me. When I understood what it took for them to get to America and build a better life, that emboldened me to stay the course in my entrepreneurial endeavors.

Guard Your Reputation

I've often thought about the captain of the ship that Isaac and his family sailed on. Talk about pressure. How many times did he need to be at his best during the hazardous trip? In the same way, you—as the owner/entrepreneur—need to be at your best when the pressure is greatest.

I've talked about the reality of being challenged by an extremely competitive and fast-changing world. Your seas will get rough, but there will be calm periods when you can shore up the skills and systems to help you and your team mature and be ready for the challenges that lie ahead.

Whether things are going well or not as good as you hoped for, this is the time to be sure that you abide by your values. If you violate your key principles, the culture that you desire and work hard to establish will have a gapping inconsistency. Recovery may never be possible.

Resist cutting an ethical corner to make a buck or keep the doors open. A reputation that can take years to build can also be lost in an instant. I could give you dozens of examples from the political and entertainment world, but I'll focus on the corporate arena.

Goldman Sachs, an American multinational finance company, has never recovered its good name after the subprime mortgage bubble burst in 2008. Comcast can't shake a horrible service reputation. Volkswagen is still stuck in the mud after deliberately designing its vehicles to circumvent emissions tests. Looking back further, the Enron scandal that took down the energy company in 2001 led to the dissolution of its accounting firm, Arthur Andersen, which was the world's fifth-largest accounting firm at the time. In better days, Arthur Andersen set ethical standards for the entire profession, which is ironic considering their downfall.

Now that you're a small business, I want you to give serious consideration to bringing on a coach or mentor. I also want you to organize an advisory board, if you have not already done so. Along with strong governance oversight of your business, these additional resources can help you stay focused on today's goals and assist you in thinking strategically about the future. They can offer suggestions on how you can optimize your performance and help you process difficult options and trade-offs. Be sure to tap into their expertise when navigating difficult waters. They have loads of professional experience that you can draw upon.

Be sure to also put on your listening ears. Pay attention to how well you listen to your coaches, mentors, and advisors. Listen to what your employees have to say, but be especially attentive to the person who knows you the best—your spouse or partner. So much wisdom can come from your inner circle when tackling problems and developing options. Going it alone is never a good idea. Listen more, talk less!

Unfortunately, I've known entrepreneurs with small to mid-sized businesses who have an advisory board but failed to involve them when facing key decisions. It's like they didn't want to admit they needed help. Don't fall into that trap.

Here's another reason you don't want to make decisions in a vacuum: stress can make the mind do funny things. When you're under pressure, your body can kick off all sorts of unwise reactions. Be aware when your emotions are helter-skelter. Slow down and reach out to those who have your best interests in mind.

One time, I witnessed an entrepreneur who made an unwise decision to sell his company in the heat of the moment. He did so without involving his board. That was a shame as well as a costly mistake because this entrepreneur was fleeced by the vultures who swept in and took his company on the cheap. His advisory board could have helped him evaluate the offer and advised him on how to sell his company without giving the store away.

Never discount what your spouse might offer as advice. While there are emotional, mental, and physical differences between the sexes—I say "vive la difference"—it's worth noting that men and women bring different strengths to the table in the business world. Men, generally speaking, tend to be more competitive and derive self-esteem from their job or their position, while women often have a deeper interest in people and feelings as well as building relationships. Women also have greater intuitive awareness than men. While there are exceptions to these generalizations, these differences often hold true. The key is to listen and benefit from these differing strengths, be they manifest in males or females.

I say all this as a preamble to the worst hiring decision I made in my life. It all started when I lost a company president for a firm that had outgrown the president's ability to manage and lead.

After he resigned, I knew I was looking for a new president with a certain skill set and experience in a specific area of business.

After an exhaustive process, I believed I had found an individual who had all the right credentials. He had great experience in the exact field I was looking for, and he interviewed well over the phone. The next step was asking him and his wife to visit our company so that we could check him out and he could check us out. After showing them around for much of a day, we had plans to have dinner together at a nice restaurant, which is the relaxed part of the exploration/interview process. In those situations, I make it a point to have Doris join me.

On the drive over to the restaurant, I told Doris, "I think he's the one. He seems perfect for the job. He has all the right experience I'm looking for. You're going to like him."

We had an enjoyable evening, although there were a couple of awkward moments. Maybe something off-color was said or he revealed a little too much detail—we call it TMI or too much information today—but Doris was not enamored with him at all.

After we'd said our goodbyes and were on our way home, Doris—who rarely interferes with my evaluations—said, "Honey, I know you think this is your person, but there is something about him that just doesn't feel right to me."

"Oh? Can you put your finger on anything?"

"I can't, but something was off about him."

This was her intuition talking, which I discounted. I tend to think logically: the right experience, the right background, the right age—what was there not to like? My mind was made up. "I think he's perfect for the job," I said.

"Okay, if that's the way you feel, then so be it, but I'm just telling you how I feel." And then Doris let the matter drop.

If I had only listened to my dear wife. But I didn't listen to other managers who interacted with him during the interview process either. Several said they didn't jell with him, but they weren't specific.

Well, given what I just shared, it should come as no surprise that my hire for the company president was a disaster.

Soon after he came on board, the company started losing money. Employee morale slipped. Six months later, key senior managers were leaving for greener pastures. The company culture, which was aligned well at the start of his tenure, was in shambles.

I had to fire him, which was difficult and costly. I began another presidential search, but it took time to rebuild employee morale and regain sales momentum.

I could have saved myself a lot of grief if I had listened to my wife and managers.

It pays to listen, so work on your listening skills. You can check on how you're doing by asking yourself: "Am I listening to understand, or am I listening to reply?"

Listening is also a good check on your ego. A strong leader with ego needs will often dominate conversation and has trouble being a good listener. God gave us two ears and one mouth for a reason.

I've even seen this trait play out in the boardroom a number of times. The president of the company, surrounded by his board of directors, takes command of the room. It's all about him (or her): he's the only voice in the room, the only one with an opinion. His desire for control, fueled by a strong ego and high self-esteem, resulted in him talking and talking and telling and telling, all the while failing to tap into the wisdom around his table.

I've also served on boards where presidents with some of these tendencies had to hear that they would be better served if they focused on listening more and talking less. (You should have been a fly on the wall to witness the tactful way this was said.) We usually couched this along the lines of becoming a better leader by having a "personal desire to improve" by showing a "willingness to listen." Or, if blunter language was called for, how they could be listening more and talking less. The ability to listen means the ability to take in more information, we'll say.

Adding Capacity

A good board of directors will also help presidents as their business grows and the breadth of operations expands. As more employees are added to increase the professionalism and specialization needs required by the entrepreneurial business, maintaining the culture of the organization becomes more challenging, especially if you expand your territory into other states and have to open satellite offices. How can you maintain the company culture and values when this happens?

That's a great question. When SuperNet grew rapidly in the mid-1990s, there were periods when we added thirty-to-forty employees monthly. We were also acquiring other ISPs, and when we joined together with seventeen other ISPs into one new company and went public on NASDAQ in the spring of 1999, we had to change our headquarters three times so that we could find the necessary employee talent. (Our last headquarters was in Reston, Virginia, which was only five miles from AOL's national headquarters, so there was a lot of talent in the area.)

That being said, we had to find new ways and work harder than ever to retain our desired corporate culture when we had 1,500 employees in numerous states. That was a lot different than when we started with forty-six employees in one location in Lancaster.

We had to integrate values statements into new employee orientation, define our cultural values as we negotiated for acquiring companies, and develop posters to display in lunchrooms and lobbies, such as this example:

OneMain.com's Core Values and Beliefs

1. We respect the individual and believe that individuals who are treated with respect and given responsibility respond by giving their best.

2. We require complete honesty and integrity in everything we do.

3. We make commitments with care and then live up to them. In all things, we do what we say we are going to do.

4. Work is an important part of life, and it should be fun. Being a good business person does not mean being stuffy and boring.

5. We love to compete, and we believe that competition brings out the best in us.

6. Clarity is understanding our mission, our values, and our goals, and what we expect from each other is critical to any success.

7. We are frugal. We guard and conserve the company's resources with at least the same vigilance that we would guard and conserve any of our personal resources.

8. We feel a sense of urgency on any matters related to any customers. We air problems and we are always responsive. We are customer-driven.

9. We insist on giving our best effort in everything we undertake.

10. We are believers in the Golden Rule. In all our dealings, we will strive to be friendly and courteous, as well as fair and compassionate.

That's quite a list! These were some of the techniques we incorporated to publicize and promote our values and culture.

For me, one of the biggest tests of stating our values and the culture we desired came unexpectedly when we assembled our group of seventeen company owners and presidents in Washington, D.C. for our "Founders Conference." This was when we took a big step in putting together our plans to "roll-up" seventeen ISPs into a new public company.

We, as founders, along with the investment bankers, would be explaining our business plan and the process of going public on NASDAQ. The Founders Meeting would also be the first assembly of our future management team, so this was a really important meeting in many ways.

The night before the event, as folks were flying in, I, along with Rod and Carlton, did a dry run of the program content with several investment bankers. We showed them our PowerPoint presentation that we would use the following day when everyone would be in attendance.

As part of our PowerPoint presentation, I included a section on the importance of company culture with a slide showing "Our Five Guiding Principles" along with these five bullet points:

• **People**—we will treat people (our employees, customers, and suppliers) with fairness and respect.

• **Quality**—we will consistently and continuously exceed the expectations of our customers.

• **Integrity**—we will deal honestly and fairly with all people in all of our business relationships.

• **Mutuality**—we will work for the mutual success of our employees, customers, and shareholders.

• **Innovation**—we will develop innovative solutions to meet our customers' needs.

One of the leading investment bankers cornered me after the presentation. "Good job," he said, "but you have to take that soft @#$% out. Wall Street isn't interested in that. The investors only care about company strategy and the numbers. You need to be focusing on the ROI," he said, referring to return on investment.

Did he say *soft @#$%*? I wasn't going to take that lying down. "I don't consider what we value in people as soft @#$%," I said, using the same earthy term. "Our company culture and our core values are an important part of what we stand for. I consider these five values to be a very important part of who we are and what we want to do here."

Later that evening, I told Rod and Carlton about my conversation with the investment banker. I made it clear that I wasn't going to budge on this—I was drawing a line in the sand. But I wanted to hear from them.

"What do you think?" I asked.

Rod and Carlton didn't hesitate. "It's still our company, not Wall Street's," my son said.

"And we still have control of the PowerPoint," Carlton added.

They were behind me 100 percent. So, we left the slide in.

I'll never forget what happened when I shared our "Five Guiding Principles" on the screen in the Watergate Hotel meeting room in our nation's capital. I shot a glance at the investment banker who told us to leave it out. He was standing in the back of the meeting room, fit to be tied. An angry look filled his face, and his neck was as red as a cherry tomato. He was ticked.

I didn't gloss over the values slide and move on. No, I took my time explaining the importance of culture and why every company needed guiding values such as these five. Although I was nervous, I was also grateful we had left the slide in because it was the right thing to do.

When our presentation ended and we took a break, three different ISP presidents or company owners crowded around me, sharing how much they appreciated that values slide.

"That's the kind of company we want to be a part of," said one.

"Those values are pretty cool stuff," chimed in another.

Not one person approached me to talk about ROI. I felt vindicated and experienced an inner peace.

The point here is so important that I'm going to use all capital letters: DO NOT BE AFRAID TO SHARE VALUES THAT ARE IMPORTANT TO YOU AND YOUR COMPANY!

A Final Point

If, after you launch your business, things are moving swimmingly, enjoy the ride. But don't become overconfident. Instead, keep a continued focus on strengthening culture and communication. Remind yourself to listen, especially when you think you have all the answers.

As your business grows and you develop a track record and performance history, place a renewed emphasis on your relationship with your investors and bankers. Develop regular communication patterns with them, just as you would with your board of directors (if you have one). I encourage quarterly meetings with your bankers, which is the way you build understanding of strategy and relationships.

This is all part of setting up an environment where you are meeting regularly with your board, your advisors, and your investors.

There's nothing like face time and what it can accomplish.

EIGHT

Anchoring at Sea

"The primary asset of any business is its organization. I like business because it is competitive. Business keeps books. The books are the scorecards. Profit is the measure of accomplishment, not the ideal measure, but the most practical that can be devised."

—William Feather, author and publisher of
The William Feather Magazine, a publication
filled with his business-centric "featherisms"

"Only those who dare to fail greatly can ever achieve greatly."

—Robert F. Kennedy, U.S. senator and
brother of President John F. Kennedy

"You won't get it right if you don't commit to keep trying."

—unknown

L et's talk about what happens if business is good—or better than expected—during the first year of operation.

I know what you're thinking: *I sure hope I have that problem. Bring it on!*

Better-than-expected business—or too much sales activity—is a great problem to have, but I don't want you to view this development as a "problem." I'd rather that you view a strong, out-of-the-gate start as a *challenge* because you and your new company will have your work cut out for you to keep up with the unforeseen volume of activity.

Systems that worked initially—like simple recordkeeping on Excel spreadsheets or accounting software like QuickBooks—will start to bog down under the increasing volume of data. Things that made sense to do manually at a certain level won't make sense any longer, so you're going to have to find a way to automate and integrate.

In case you're wondering, combinations of Excel spreadsheets and QuickBooks are not integrated. It's also been my experience that an Information Technology (IT) system built internally doesn't interface well with a new one. Worse than that, your growing IT needs will probably require manual entry of data multiple times, which is both redundant and costly in labor. I must also add that mistakes happen each time new fingers do the data entry, so add human error to the list.

My recommendation: look into third-party providers who can build computerized systems that are fully integrated between sales, accounting, and operations for less cost than you can do it with your internal IT staff. You will need to check out these companies as soon as possible because increasing your ability to analyze multiple data points and apply analytics will optimize your business and help you to grow and/or maintain market share against your competition.

In many new start-ups, the founding entrepreneurs have grown step-by-step with the firm, and while they may be able to operate on an intuitive basis from their knowhow and memory, that's not so easy when the company grows—especially rapidly. As the company grows in complexity, it becomes increasingly difficult for the incoming managers, or the next generation of hires, to operate on a similar basis.

For the firm to move to the next level of size or provide the same breadth of services and products, streamlined systems become essential. You'll also see that the specialization of staff becomes the norm, meaning people are hired into one department for one job, like someone who's background is in human resources, or has worked on the IT side, or comes from a sales and marketing background. In the early days, I'm sure your first few employees performed multiples tasks; that's normal in start-ups. But as you and your company grow, so does the need for employees with key experience in those positions.

Firms that fail to make this transition from the "entrepreneurial stage" to a more sophisticated "professional management" approach will encounter challenges in the marketplace from more efficient competitors. They will also encounter succession challenges.

Let me share this illustration. One time, I consulted with a father-and-son team in which the founder developed a successful firm that sold various goods and delivered them with a fleet of company trucks. Over time, one of their better margin specialties was dealing in polymer—or plastics. The founder, whom I'll call Jerry, started a niche business by purchasing thirteen different grades of polymer in bulk and redistributing the plastic material in smaller quantities when customers needed a certain grade of polymer. The polymer grade needed for manufacturing a garbage bag is a dollar less than the high-grade polymer used for producing a CD. Jerry developed an excellent business and ran it well, but most of the knowledge of how the company operated was in his head. He had a great nose for going after business and was gifted at closing the sale.

His son Ricky started working for him in high school but went off to college. Following graduation, he stayed in school two more years to earn his MBA. When he had his master's degree in hand, he came back to his father's business and immediately saw the need to develop systems. He could see that many employees were running around like chickens with their heads cut off because they weren't sure what to do. Or they were waiting around to drive a load to a customer because their trucks hadn't been loaded—a classic case of the left hand not knowing what the right hand was doing.

Jerry thought much of Ricky's "re-arranging" was unnecessary. "Just get out there and sell," Jerry said. "You don't need a computer to schedule the drivers. Just assign them their regular delivery routes and let them adjust according to their load. They'll get it done."

Ricky rolled his eyes whenever he heard his father say stuff like that. He thought his father wasted too much time schmoozing customers instead of closing the deal and moving on to the next one.

The tension between father and son rose to a level where their frustrations were sky high. When I met with them for the first time, Ricky was seriously thinking about exiting the business.

I was still figuring out the situation when something interesting happened. The father-and-son firm purchased a similar business two states away, but this company utilized more automation in scheduling and accounting areas—the total opposite of what Jerry had done for decades.

The light went on for the father, who came to the realization that Ricky's new skill sets from his MBA would be essential to run a larger multi-state operation. A new dawn had arrived.

They were smart—and looked to me to develop a succession plan where the father would gradually turn over the business to his son and then head off into the sunset to enjoy retirement while his son would transition the business into a more efficient operation.

I'm happy to report that a good family business was saved.

Encourage Innovation

Every company needs to give a high priority to improving the way they conduct business. When new technology can dramatically increase productivity or improve quality, then it needs to be adopted into your operation. If you don't, you run the risk of not being competitive over the long run.

Many companies develop what I call "Continuous Improvement Programs," or CIP, to encourage innovation. In the 1980s and '90s, this was a particularly popular practice because of the teaching and writings of quality guru Edwards Deming, who came up with fourteen key principles that every business should follow. The points were first presented in Deming's 1982 book, *Out of the Crisis*, and they are still relevant thirty-five years later. Here's a quick overview of the fourteen points:

1. Create constancy of purpose toward the improvement of the product and service. Your aim should be to become competitive, stay in business, and provide jobs.

2. Know that you're in a new economic age. Management must awaken to the challenge of today, learn their responsibilities, and take on leadership for change.

3. Cease your dependence on inspection to achieve quality. You can eliminate the need for inspection on a mass basis by building quality into the product in the first place.

4. End the practice of awarding business on the basis of a price tag. Instead, what you want to do is minimize total cost. Move toward a single supplier for any one item, and forge a long-term relationship of loyalty and trust.

5. Improve constantly and forever the system of production and service, which will improve quality and productivity, and thus constantly decrease costs.

6. Institute on-the-job training.

7. You can institute leadership by understanding that the aim of leadership should be to help people and machines and gadgets do a better job.

8. Drive out fear in the ranks, so that everyone can work effectively for the company.

9. Break down barriers between departments. People in research, design, sales, and production must work as a team and foresee problems in production.

10. Eliminate slogans and exhortations for "zero defects" or "new levels of productivity" with your work force. Quotas on the factory floor are never a good idea. Substitute leadership.

11. Remove barriers that rob the hourly worker of his right to pride of workmanship.

12. Remove barriers that rob people in management of their right to pride of workmanship.

13. Institute a vigorous program of education and self-improvement. A better-educated employee is a better employee.

14. Put everybody in the company to work to accomplish a transformation. That means the transformation of the company is everybody's job.

Basically, Deming taught firms to eliminate massive quality inspection teams by building statistical quality control into the manufacturing system, with the production workers directly responsible for monitoring their quality. Companies who failed to keep pace with quality and productivity improvements, or lacked innovation, would fall behind as other firms implemented new ideas to improve their products and services.

A great example of falling behind the curve happened to Holiday Inn, which had a huge lead as the preferred lodging provider along the U.S. Interstate Highway System back in the late 1950s and 1960s, the early days of interstate travel and the heyday of postwar family tourism. Before air travel became common-place, families packed up their station wagons and pet dog and hit the open road to Grandma's place or drove to Mount Rushmore and the Grand Canyon to see the sights—and stayed in Holiday Inns along the way. Starting out with several dozen hotels in the mid-1950s, the hotel chain grew to over 1,000 Holiday Inns by 1968.

The joke was that there was a Holiday Inn at every interstate exit in America, and the company boasted that 96 percent of all U.S. travelers stayed at a Holiday Inn at least once. With consist-ently clean rooms and a pool for the kids, Holiday Inns were a hit. Rooms were affordable. Children stayed for no extra charge.

But as air travel got cheaper and Baby Boomers became adults, Holiday Inn let the quality of their operations slip. Holiday Inn grew so large that it became more difficult to control the condi-tions of each property. The parent company failed to develop new prototypes. They let design and standards vary. The brand was no longer consistent, so customers could not be sure of what they would get when they stayed at a Holiday Inn.

By the 1980s, Holiday Inns were as stale as a week-old English muffin. The so-called "Great Sign"—the iconic green roadside sign used by Holiday Inn in its heyday—had been sent to the scrap heap. Holiday Inn was no longer up to its calling as "The Nation's Innkeeper." Competition was coming from higher-end brands like Marriott, Hilton, and Westin and cheaper alternatives like Red Roof Inn, Days Inn, and La Quinta Inns.

Faced with having to do something, Holiday Inn underwent a housecleaning in the mid-1980s—from top to bottom. A more in-novative and disciplined team of managers developed a new hotel prototype called "Hampton Inn" that franchisee owners had to strictly follow, and they promoted a new "selected service" alter-native for traveling customers. They focused on the core things the average customer wanted: a clean, nicely appointed room; a quality bed; and a free hot breakfast in the morning—a first for a mid-price hotel in the industry. They eliminated the in-hotel restaurant and bar and placed intense focus on training the staff to provide outstanding customer service, backed up by a 100 percent satisfaction guarantee to the customer—also a first in the industry.

The new leadership team implemented an extensive quality control program, backed up by corporate inspections every six months. They tracked thirty areas of customer satisfaction every month, giving the owners feedback and benchmarks with other Hamptons. The new brand became a huge success. Today, there are over 2,000 Hamptons by Hilton and Hampton Inn and Suites in seventeen countries.

I'm alongside Calvin High and Dale High at a ribbon-cutting ceremony for the opening of High Hotel's Hampton Inn in Lancaster, Pennsylvania.

The reason I share this story is because I decided to pursue an entrepreneurial endeavor myself in 2009 when I elected to build my own Hampton Inn.

I didn't walk into the lobby blind, as they say. Back when I worked for High Industries, one of the holding companies I was in charge of was High Hotels, which invested in eight different hotels ranging from four Hampton Inns to two Homewood Suites, a Marriott Courtyard, and a Hilton Garden Inn. Overseeing eight hotels gave me a good grip on how a good hotel should operate.

What I saw is that the hotel business—like every other industry in America—had to change with the times, which leads me to an important point I want to make about any start-up business in America today. We hear a lot of talk about "diversity," and while I want to steer clear of political correctness, almost every new business will be interacting with an increasingly diverse universe of customers. There's no getting around this as the demographics of this country is changing rapidly due to immigration. You need to be thinking about how you can build a diverse team that can take advantage of reaching an increasingly diverse population. That will mean creative thinking from your hiring practices to product design to servicing your customer.

Train your people about the benefits of diversity. Encourage building a work force made up of folks from different backgrounds and cultures. Find the good in each culture that persons can bring to the organization.

And, in everything you do, keep your focus on the customer.

For me is all goes back to a core value that's been a part of every business I've been involved in: "Treating all persons with dignity."

The lesson to be learned here is this: Build stability through your company as you're able to find "anchor time." Employ better systems to help keep you competitive into the future. Encourage continuous improvement, promote innovation, and capture the benefits of diversity.

When you lift anchor and set sail again, these practices will help you cut smoothly through the water.

NINE

The Look from the Crow's Nest

"If a man can write a better book, preach a better sermon, or make a better mousetrap than his neighbor, though he builds his house in the woods, the world will make a beaten path to his door."

—Ralph Waldo Emerson, 19th century essayist,
lecturer, and poet

"Imagination is more important than knowledge. For knowledge is limited, whereas imagination embraces the entire world, stimulating progress, giving birth to evolution."

—Albert Einstein, German-born theoretical physicist

"Name the greatest of all inventors. Accident."

—Mark Twain, humorist, writer, and entrepreneur

I love quoting Mark Twain. He's one of this country's revered authors and is best known for writing *The Adventures of Huckleberry Finn*, which nearly every high school student reads some time in English class before he or she graduates.

Twain—born Samuel Clemens—was raised in Hannibal, Missouri, in the mid-1850s and became a prolific author during the last half of the 19th century. He was an inquisitive guy and inveterate traveler with a great sense of humor. He loved to tinker in his workshop. His first invention—an adjustable strap that would tighten shirts at the waist and eliminate the need for suspenders—was granted a patent by the U.S. Patent Office in 1871. The adjustable strap didn't sell like proverbial hotcakes, but Twain's books sure did. He was fascinated by new technology, especially a newfangled but clumsy configuration of rollers and spindly arms that was known as a *typewriter*. Twain was such an early adopter that he became the first person to submit a typed manuscript to a publisher.

Then he heard about the Paige Typesetter, an invention of James W. Paige that could typeset automatically and perform tasks like justification—or spacing out words in a line to maintain even right and left margins—with the help of one operator at the keyboard.

With over 18,000 separate parts, the Paige Typesetter was an incredibly complex machine for its time, which was the 1880s. Twain became Paige's financial angel, investing the bulk of his royalties from *Tom Sawyer* and *The Adventures of Huckleberry Finn* *plus* a large portion of his wife's inheritance—a total of $6 million in today's dollars.

Unfortunately for Twain, Paige could never get the darn thing to work that well, and only two prototypes were ever built. A rival automatic typesetter, known as the Mergenthaler Linotype Compositor, was far superior and grabbed the printing market.

And that's where we got linotype, a "hot metal" typesetting system that cast blocks of metal type. Book publishers and newspapers around the world purchased a Linotype machine, earning the company hundreds of millions of dollars until the 1980s when the technology was relegated to the dust bin with the invention of computerized typesetting.

As for Twain, it wasn't his fault that he lost much of his fortune when he listened to James Paige tell him that he could make his typesetting machine work. Fortunately for Twain, he had his writing career to fall back on, but what happened to the famous author is a cautionary tale. A "sure thing" idea doesn't guarantee success, and that's because the world is changing faster than ever before.

It's insanely difficult to predict what's around the corner or what will capture the public's interest, especially with the way the world has changed in the last twenty years. I'm talking about developments that no one could have predicted two decades ago: globalization and terrorism. Each situation greatly affects entrepreneurs. I'll start with globalization first.

Initially pitched as a strategy to raise living standards in rich and poor countries, globalization generally means giving developing countries access to our market so they can export lower-priced goods to our shores. Free trade is said to promote global economic growth and improve the lives of poor people since they produce jobs.

On the flip side, this presents a problem for First World countries in that jobs are lost and transferred to lower-cost countries. U.S. workers have seen their wages cut or remain stagnant because of economic pressures that threaten to export their jobs to a cheaper country.

This is why there's a huge political debate going on in this country. You, as an entrepreneur, need to watch how this "free trade" issue works out in Washington. If your entrepreneurial business is tied to bringing a product *into* this country from a land where its costs much less to make the item, then you'll want to see the globalization trend continue. If you've come up with a product or service that you want to produce in this country—and face competition from imports—then you're amiable to tariffs and government policies that are pro-business, meaning lower taxes, less regulation, and tougher trade deals.

I'm not taking sides on the free trade issue, but I am reminded of what Nobel Prize winner and free-marketer Milton Friedman once said: "Economic freedom is as vital to a free society as is political freedom."

This is where the terrorism angle comes in. There's no doubt that the impact of terrorism on the daily lives of Americans and our economy is a major concern. Gallup polling says that nine out of ten Americans say they are going about their business as usual, but another major terrorist event would send this economy on its heels. Remember how business came to a standstill after terrorists flew commercial airliners into the World Trade Center and the Pentagon on September 11, 2001? It was months, if not a year or so, before the country's economy rebounded.

Extreme events like terrorist attacks and natural disasters such as the 2011 earthquake off the coast of Japan, which triggered a powerful tsunami that killed more than 16,000 people, have the potential to psychologically impact everyone, affecting both expectations and perceptions. The silver lining for entrepreneurs is these events neither encourage nor discourage entrepreneurial activity, according to those who study the impact of terrorism and natural disasters. Ironically, these events at times can provide for new opportunities.

Using data from forty-three countries during the post-9/11 years from 2002 to 2005, researcher Tilman Brück of the Institute for the Study of Labor in Bonn, Germany, said, "We find that terrorist attacks have a positive and significant impact on entrepreneurial activity. The disruption of customary habits and the weakening of traditional institutions create opportunities and may change the balance of power in favor of smaller, more flexible organizations."

Whatever happens in the future regarding terrorism and natural disaster cannot be predicted. All we know is that *something* will happen, and how the market reacts cannot be predicted. In some manner, events around the world will impact you because we co-exist today in a global economy. That will not change.

This is why I want you to include "risk management" as part of your entrepreneurial effort. A good entrepreneur has the ability to accurately understand and manage risk.

There's a popular misconception that entrepreneurs are daredevils, always looking for another cliff—or business opportunity—to run off of. That's not who I want you to be. I want you to coolly and responsibly weigh the pros and cons of starting up and seeing through your entrepreneurial venture. Keep these ideas in mind:

• You never want to bet more than you can lose.

• You have a Plan B in the wings, and it's not a bad idea to have contingency ideas drawn up for Plans C and D.

• Expect "Murphy's Law" to rear its ugly head, meaning what could go wrong will go wrong.

• Remind yourself that there's a direct relationship between risk and reward. Many times, the greater the potential upside, the greater the risks involved. Winning entrepreneurs achieve success through keen awareness and management of risks.

You must include risk management as a critical component of your Annual Plan and your multi-year Strategic Plan. For example, backing up your computer isn't the sexiest part of planning, but with an increasing dependency on digitally generated and stored information to run your business, you will need some form of back-up for your computer-driven data. Thus, the importance of having a redundant source—such as a backup off-site that's "in the cloud"—mitigates the risk of losing data critical to your business.

I served on the board of an insurance company that put extensive time and cost into the backup of its data and operating systems so that they would be assured an on-going ability to continue running its business in the event of a fire or terrorism at the company's main headquarters. That's the way you manage risk—by getting out in front of it.

The explosion of technology that drives a more rapid rate of change demands that you stay current with developing technologies. Sometimes events happen at hyper speed that an entire market gets overturned like an apple cart. Called "disruptive change," a term introduced in the mid-1990s by Clayton M. Christensen, a Harvard professor who wrote the book, *The Innovator's Dilemma: When New Technologies Cause Great Firms to Fail*, this type of unexpected change can leave industry leaders in the dust if they react too slowly to new technological breakthroughs.

My favorite example of disruptive technology is what happened to the Eastman Kodak Co. If you were born after the Eighties, you probably have no idea what a "Kodak moment" is, but that was a phrase used for taking a memorable picture of someone at a particularly adorable moment in time.

Back in the days of still photography, taking photographs was a form of delayed gratification. First, you inserted a roll of Kodak film into your Brownie camera and took photographs sparingly since it cost good money to process and produce a photo from each twenty-four- or thirty-six-picture roll. That's *after* you dropped the roll off at the local drugstore or put the roll into a mailer. You usually had to wait five to seven days to see your pictures.

Kodak wasn't the only company making film in the world, but they sure cornered the market after George Eastman founded the company in 1886 with the invention of roll film, which almost single-handedly brought photography to the masses. By 1976,

Kodak sold 90 percent of the photographic film in the U.S. along with 85 percent of the cameras, like the Instamatic.

A year earlier—in 1975!—a Kodak engineer named Steven Sasson invented the digital camera with a resolution of 0.1 megapixels. The thing was as big as a toaster, needed twenty seconds to take a low-quality image, and required complicated connections to a television if you wanted to see your fuzzy photo, but the basic idea was there.

In Kodak's situation, the gigantic company wasn't nimble enough—and too set in its corporate ways—to get its act together. Over the next twenty-five years, Kodak tried to produce a digital camera that matched the performance of traditional film, which was too costly for the average consumer. Kodak's DCS-100 camera cost $20,000, which was insane. Who could afford a $20k camera for taking family photos at the seashore?

Meanwhile, Canon and Sony rushed into the vacuum with simpler "point-and-shoot" digital cameras, and Kodak was left in the dust. The company filed for bankruptcy in 2012, sold off its patents, and re-emerged as a vastly different—and smaller—company in 2013.

The landscape is littered with stories similar to Kodak:

• Blockbuster video stores disappeared when Netflix started delivering DVDs by mail. Then Netflix had to re-invent itself with its huge move into digital streaming and has re-invented itself a third time by producing their own movies and original film series like *House of Cards, The Crown*, and *Orange Is the New Black*.

• Record stores disappeared along with vinyl albums, although there's been a vinyl revival in recent years.

• Swiss watchmakers were slow to adopt digital technology for their famous watches.

- Independent bookstores are nearly gone, although you can usually find one in major cities. Amazon and the rise of ebooks decimated the brick-and-mortar stores.
- Wikipedia destroyed *Encyclopedia Britannica* overnight.
- Xerox didn't capitalize on its invention of the mouse, the laser printer, or the graphical user interface.
- Nokia and BlackBerry are afterthoughts today in the smartphone arena.

Speaking of smartphones, the big makers of digital cameras saw *their* bottoms lines take a huge hit after Apple added a camera to the iPhone upon its introduction in 2007. In a selfie world, who needed a digital camera for a "Kodak moment" when your smartphone takes great photos and can be immediately uploaded to your social media portals in mere seconds?

So now the picture-printing companies took a huge hit since there was no reason to print pictures since they were going straight to Facebook and mobile phone apps such as WhatsApp.

Call this development Disrupter 2.0.

When it comes to technology, if you're not running at the front of the pack, you could get left in the dust in a hurry. I sit on the board of a manufacturing firm that has seen its multi-million-dollar Internet sales level explode to 40 percent of its volume in just a few years. Had this company not learned to market and distribute via e-commerce, they would be struggling.

Innovation—which I describe as the development of new or improved products, new methods, or new ways to serve—becomes even more critical as product life cycles shorten, often due to the rate of technological change.

Woodstream Corp., a company headquartered near Lancaster, had to literally build a better mousetrap. Even though the company has manufactured mousetraps for more than one hundred years, Woodstream had to innovate when rival companies started producing electronic rodent traps that zapped the critters when lured into a trap sprinkled with dry pet food. People prefer to dispose of dead mice and rats in this way—and not deal with an icky wooden mousetrap oozing with blood and guts.

Woodstream is an example of a legacy company that understands the necessity of constantly innovating. Another company I work with has a lofty goal as well: making 25 percent of its sales from new products that they've invented in the last three years.

That's the way you stay in business today.

Watch Out for Rapid Growth

Have you ever heard of a company growing so fast that they went bankrupt?

I have—many times, even though it would seem that demand like that should be good news, not bad.

Well, good solid growth is usually good news, but it's very important to understand the capital and cash flow requirements that rapid growth will require. Hopefully, rapid growth will enable you to make and maintain a good operating margin, but in today's rush to optimize a "window of opportunity"—where obtaining market share is deemed critical to long-term survival—it will be essential to have sufficient cash on hand to support capital and working capital needs.

Let me give you a simple illustration:

Let's say your firm has $1 million in annual sales. The cost of sales is 80 percent with a nice final profit margin of 10 percent and sixty days, on average, until you collect on your sales.

On the surface, this looks pretty good. But now assume that your market suddenly explodes to $2 million in sales. With an 80 percent cost of sales and only thirty days to pay your vendors, you will need $800,000 more for your raw materials, which take some time to manufacture into your product. This is what's known as "inventory in process."

Then the finished goods may sit in inventory a few days or weeks, which is "finished goods inventory." Then once you do sell it, you don't collect your money for another sixty days after your sale, which is known as accounts receivable, but not cash yet.

To support this type of rapid growth, you will need hundreds of thousands of dollars more in what we call "working capital." And you're not done yet. You may need to purchase more equipment to support this growth, which means the need for cash multiplies.

Maybe this illustration gives you a better understanding of the proclamation: "Cash is king!"

While poor growth and no margin are even worse problems to be facing, it's important to remember that good times and rapid growth require excellent forecasting of cash requirements and managing cash flow. Scenarios such as this emphasize how important it is to work closely with your bank and other funding sources so that adequate cash is always available for the needs of the business. You don't want to surprise your banker or investors, even with extraordinary growth.

Just in Case . . .

And while no one likes to contemplate their mortality, you need to account for succession planning for the future, both for potential management transitions as well as ownership transition, for your entrepreneurial business to move forward.

A good succession plan works to identify who would be able to manage a function in your business, if the existing manager were to become incapacitated. God forbid, but the succession plan should have a short-term person identified for such a tragedy as well a long-term plan for who could be developed for the position. This is especially important for the CEO and senior management positions within the company.

I have been involved in six public companies and seventeen private companies, and while public companies are appropriate in some industries, I have a strong preference for family-run businesses for many reasons. That said, this area of succession planning is more critical in a family business because three important aspects must be addressed, all of which need careful attention, for on-going continuity as a family business. These three aspects are:

1. Management succession
2. Ownership succession
3. Estate planning

The needs—both financial and emotional—of the "out-going" generation need to be understood and carefully planned for, while the desire and passion for the business, including the many management and ownership issues, need to be planned for by the "in-coming" generation.

My consulting is often focused on helping both out-going and in-coming generations develop successful succession plans. Just as each business is different, each family situation is different as well as estate issues. That is why I thoroughly enjoy this part of my consulting since there's no "one size fits all" component to succession planning because no two companies are alike.

My greatest joy is when a family business successfully transitions to the next generation smoothly and orderly—just as we drew it up. The statistics of family business succession are not great, but I have had the honor of working with family business succession into the third and fourth generations.

I served on the board of a very successful company that was going through the succession from the third to the fourth generation whereby the third-generation owners (two brothers and a sister) each had a child learning/working in the business, but the fourth generation had little capital to acquire the company.

The first thing I suggested was for Generation 4 to sit in on the board meetings for a couple of years to learn more about the governance of the company. Then, with the blessing from their parents, they met with an advisor to develop a proposed future management structure that defined the CEO and other roles they would assume. Then they proposed a consulting package for each of their parents and a fifteen-year buy-out, which the parents accepted on a note with interest.

When the 2009-2012 recession hit, however, the company struggled, and the parents helped by loaning some money back to the company. Now, with a recovering economy, the company is doing very well again, and another family business has successfully transitioned to the next generation. If only such cooperation within families was always the case.

The lesson to be learned here is this: even when things seem to be sailing along quite well, don't let your guard down. Continue careful risk assessment, keep an eye on disruptive technologies, manage cash flow, develop contingency plans, and even begin thinking about succession plans for the short term as well as the long term.

TEN

When the Little Boat Transforms

"But innovation is more than a new method. It is a new view of the universe, as one of risk rather than of change or certainty. It is a new view of man's role in this universe; he creates order by taking risk. And this means that innovation, rather than being an assertion of human power, is an acceptance of human responsibility."

—Peter Drucker, consultant and educator on the foundations of the modern business corporation

"Without change there is no innovation, creativity, or incentive for improvement. Those who initiate change will have a better opportunity to manage the change that is inevitable."

—William Pollard, physicist and Episcopal priest

Many of today's business opportunities are idea- and technology-driven because the Internet has made connecting with small niches of customers all over the world much easier, and hence less costly. This is where entrepreneurs can shine. If you can come up with an outstanding product or a new service, your market may not be limited to your neighborhood or even your city. The world is your oyster.

Another trend I'm following is how today's businesses have the potential for becoming multiple locations—known as franchising—when in the hands of capable entrepreneurs. These days, we're seeing franchises in all sorts of industries, from hotels to food to retirement home services. You can find thousands of independently owned franchisees across thousands of different businesses—just look at the ads in *Franchise* magazine. So opportunity abounds for entrepreneurs, either with a fresh idea or as a new franchisee.

Sometimes, though, there is a "window of opportunity" when a new idea or technology comes to market that has huge economies of scale potential. In those situations, achieving leading market share becomes critical to long-term survival.

Are you old enough to remember companies like VisiCorp, TopView, or Digital Research? They were computer operating systems when Microsoft released Windows 1.0 on November 20, 1985. The reason you never heard of them is because Windows shut down the competition.

Are you old enough to remember computers made by Tandy, Commodore, and Compaq? In the late 1970s, as PCs and Apple II computers were vying for footholds in the personal computing market, this trio of computer manufacturers were in the thick of things. They didn't make it either.

When you look at eBay, Google, and Facebook, you can find examples of competitors who were neck-and-neck at one time with their competition, but one by one they fell by the wayside. eBay's first challenger was OnSale.com. Google beat back search engines like WebCrawler and AskJeeves. Facebook brushed aside MySpace, Bebo, and Friendster.

Here's my takeaway: compared to the Industrial Age, you have to have a "winner takes all" mentality in the Information Age. If you don't reach for the brass ring when you can, you might not get another chance on the merry-go-round of business.

Most of the time, you have to fight for every foot of advancement in the brutal world of commerce. Just because Amazon is the 800-pound gorilla doesn't mean you have no chance or that you could never compete against the purchasing power of Walmart or Target. If you've identified your target market, figured out a way to reach that market and how you can personalize your business to separate you from your competition, you can be very successful on a smaller scale. Never forget that personal service is not easily duplicated by a larger organization.

If your idea is big, however, and requires scale or speed to tap into the market, you will need to rapidly add expertise and capacity to your business plan. Unless you're sitting on a stockpile of cash, you will also have to seek out major funding sources to compete in your market.

I've had experience in both situations. First, I'll start with my smaller entrepreneurial efforts such as a single-location franchised hotel, a single-market self-storage business, and a sole proprietor consulting business. These are examples of businesses that could survive and be competitive on a stand-alone basis, but they could also be expanded one additional unit at a time, if desired. Small real estate investments are another common example and are a wise long-term investment for many.

Other endeavors, however, have to keep pace with growing demand or the economies of scale will render them uncompetitive. I saw this happen with SuperNet, the ISP company that I started with my son Rod and Carlton Miller in 1993. After two years of operation, the Internet explosion demanded rapid growth: we either had to gobble up other companies or risk being gobbled up by aggressive sharks in the water. At the time, we were among the 5,000 Internet Service Providers that started up in a five-year time frame from 1993 to 1998 to meet the rocketing demand. Within five years, nearly everyone disappeared or was swallowed up—including SuperNet—as huge economies of scale came into play.

I described our amazing tale in the opening chapter, but let me give you a real-world example of how we raised capital and maneuvered through many steps to keep pace with this Internet opportunity. This is what I call "the rest of the story," as radio commentator Paul Harvey used to say years ago.

When we launched SuperNet, the three of us put in $10,000 each for routers, computers, and working capital. Within two months, Rod was convinced that our ISP business would be huge, so he resigned from his good banking job, which, as a father, made me rather nervous. Carlton and I put in some additional capital, and my son worked for a less-than-market pittance, earning "sweat equity" to maintain his one-third ownership.

As we grew by leaps and bounds, we needed more working capital so we could purchase more routers and move into a larger building. Banks, however, weren't eager to lend money in an industry that had no track record.

Since we couldn't get a bank loan, we husbanded our resources carefully until one day a person I'll call Larry poked around and asked questions about what we were doing. He had some ideas of his own, including putting certain educational content on the Internet. He told us that he was willing to invest in our company because he believed in us.

Rod, Carlton, and I looked at each other, and we were thinking the same thing: *We need his money.* In exchange for his investment, we sold him a 25 percent share of SuperNet, which was the first leveraged moment of our start-up venture. We used Larry's money to purchase more routers and move into a bigger building, which allowed us to go after more customers since we could successfully service them.

A few months later, Larry said he needed the money he invested in SuperNet for another opportunity. Would we be willing to buy back his interest for the same amount he invested?

Once again, this was slam-dunk idea because his request basically meant we got to use his money interest-free for several months. Once we returned his investment, though, we had to stretch our money and be very careful how we spent our budget. Once again, we were all in. Looking back, we were fortunate things worked out this way because we got 25 percent of the company back—a piece of the company that would be worth many millions of dollars just eight years later.

About the same time we said goodbye to Larry as an investor, we received an inquiry from the local phone company, whose phone lines we were using for the dial-up service. Our local phone company had decided they wanted to jump into the Internet business and determined that SuperNet was, by far, their best entry into the industry since we were the leader in the local market.

Rod, Carlton, and I huddled together. We agreed that we had a winning idea and told the local phone company that we were not for sale.

Then things got real interesting. The local phone company said, *Fine, we'll start our own ISP and directly compete against you guys.*

We knew the local phone company had deep pockets. We also looked at our financials, and they were not pretty. We were running out of capital, and none of us had any more money from our personal accounts to invest, so we had to come up with a plan.

In the end, we called the local phone company and offered to sell them a 50 percent share of SuperNet for $500,000 as well as a commitment to fund the next half-million dollars in capital. We also asked the local phone company to let us use some of their telephonic equipment that was excess capacity—equipment that we would otherwise need to purchase.

They took the deal. Upon the signing of the contract, we formed a six-member board of directors: the three of us and the three of them. Better yet, the local phone company inserted our Internet marketing materials into their monthly statements, which numbered in the tens of thousands.

Here's what I want to say in boldface type: Even though we gave up half of our company, we felt that we got a very good deal. Sometimes merging with a strategic partner and collaborating can be an excellent way to survive and obtain critical resources or capital if you are a small company with a big idea.

We worked well together with the local phone company, holding monthly board meetings. With the chance to include a promotional piece in their monthly statements, we received a big jolt of new business. We expanded our territory, took on more customers, and acquired smaller ISPs. Our economies of scale were excellent as we could often fold the customers we acquired into our existing T3 network. (I described in Chapter 1 how T3 telephone lines had ten times the capacity of a T1 telephone line but was only three times the cost.)

Then I recalled how, when I was working for High Industries in the mid-1980s,

I was responsible for a media company that got into the cable business. We started acquiring small cable operators in second-tier markets in Kentucky, North Carolina, Maryland, and Pennsylvania. The first thing we did was consolidate the back-of-the-house operations, add programming, and increase the price, but we tried to not change anything that touched the consumer. We even kept the small offices in these towns, where people could still come for technical support, ask questions, or pay their bill.

As I watched our SuperNet business continue double-digit growth from month to month, I felt this same cable business model could be applied to the Internet market. That's when I took a long weekend at our cottage on the Chesapeake Bay and wrote an eighteen-page business plan that outlined how we could acquire more ISPs in secondary markets along the Atlantic Seaboard and produce a noteworthy Eastern regional ISP company that could be taken public on NASDAQ.

I had taken some companies public in the last few years, so I knew investment bankers in New York and SEC (Securities and Exchange Commission) attorneys in Washington D.C. Based upon my acquaintance with a dozen movers and shakers, I thought I could pull off an IPO—initial public offering—given my networking contacts.

I reviewed the plan with Rod and Carlton. They liked what they saw and supported me, so we presented my idea to our phone company partners at our next monthly board meeting.

Well, I was certainly naïve! I thought our local phone company would have more of the entrepreneurial spirit, but I missed that by a country mile. They had zero interest in pursuing such a "risky opportunity" and no desire to expand into territory outside of their service area. Their decision disappointed me, which I stated for the record at the meeting. I knew that Rod and Carlton were keen on moving in that direction.

This was our first major disagreement on strategy with our 50/50 partner—and we were at a stalemate. Then the plot thickened: their three board members quickly informed us that they were interested in buying out *our* half of the company.

What should we do? After all, we didn't want to sell our half. We wanted to see if we could pursue our plan and put together a winning IPO that would solve our capital problems. But now we were facing a hostile takeover.

Feeling like we were painted into a corner, we decided the only way we would sell would be at a very high price. After all, we knew the market, and Internet IPOs were bringing very high prices.

How about $12 million for our half of the company?

The three board of directors representing the local phone company nearly choked on their morning coffee. They expressed being shocked at our valuation and basically told us to pound sand.

Okay. How about letting us put together that IPO. We could both benefit from going public.

This time our partners said we had their blessing.

We researched ISP companies of respectable size that fit our geography, and then we began visiting prospective company owners, obtaining confidentiality agreements. Within a short time, I had seven signed letters of intent.

With these documents in hand, I met with several investment bankers that I had worked with in taking five companies public in recent years. One of the investment bankers was quite excited, but he tempered his remarks. "Great strategy and plan, but what we don't need is another regional Internet provider," the investment banker said. "What you need to do is take this thing national. I'd be glad to help you find other companies."

He also suggested coming up with a strategy to become the largest ISP in secondary markets. "When the subscriber growth begins to slow down, as it will, one of the big players will come and want to acquire you to keep their growth going," he said. "This would be a four-to-five-year play."

We took this feedback to our partners at the local phone company, but they still expressed reservations; they knew the regional market but professed not to know the national market. We listened, walked through why our plan still made the most financial sense, and then presented them with a new idea: we would merge our company into a new public company, but they—our phone partners—would retain the rights and the service to the customers in their immediate telephone geography. As we would find out later, the investment bankers were not pleased to hear about this "carve-out," as it's called in financial circles, but we made the deal, and we needed to honor it.

Once things were square with our phone company partners, we made a deal with the investment banking firm to work together in identifying more companies that would merge with us and give us a national footprint. We developed an "acquisition template" so that the offers would be similar in structure and valuations and based on a number of factors: subscriber count, growth rates in subscriptions, average price per subscriber, net income trends, and balance sheet ratios.

We had to be in a hurry, which necessitated using a private jet so we could meet with as many prospects as soon as possible. One day, I remember jetting off to an early morning meeting in Florida, an afternoon meeting in Indiana, and an Ohio meeting that evening. A private jet felt like an excessive expenditure to me, but the investment bankers knew time was of essence.

In terms of the structure, we negotiated as close to a 50/50 deal as possible—50 percent cash for their business and 50 percent shares in the new public company. In most cases, the cash took care of their existing debt and loans to the business and even some return, so that the 50 percent stock was all upside.

If they had a company that was worth $6 million, based on our pricing criteria, then they would receive $3 million in cash from the money raised from our IPO as well as $3 million worth of stock in the new company. We were aiming for a $10 per share valuation in the new public company and valued their business on that expectation, which would mean they would receive 300,000 shares.

In most cases, we also offered a two-year management contract to the entrepreneur and his top team. We also required them to "stay in the deal" in case the initial "strike price" of the IPO fell as low as $8. We put this clause in the contract because we didn't want firms pulling out if we came up a bit short of our $10 price-per-share objective on the day of issue. Then again, if we were able to get more than $10 per share, that would be to their benefit, so market timing would be very important.

At our "founders conference" in Washington D.C., we ended up with seventeen companies from California to Florida to Vermont ready to partner with us on the IPO. Once that happened, we would have a national footprint of over 381,000 subscribers and 663 points of presence—or modem locations—in twenty-five states.

Once agreements were signed with these seventeen companies, the detailed work began. To show the consolidated financials in the stock-offering documents, we had to get all the charts of accounts from all the companies consistent with each other and show three years of combined financials. As you can imagine, the specific accounts and capitalization practices were different among the seventeen companies. To help us get to speed, we studied AOL's chart of accounts, since they were already public, and then we had to reconstruct three years' worth of financials for all seventeen companies, costing many hundreds of thousands of CPA-auditing dollars.

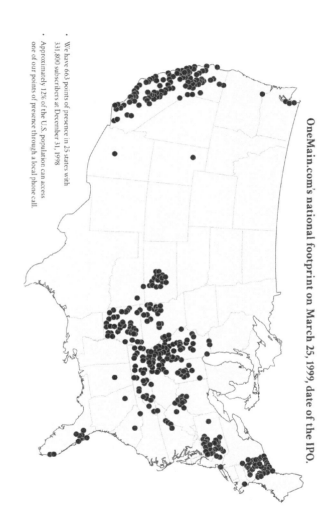

OneMain.com's national footprint on March 25, 1999, date of the IPO.

- We have 663 points of presence in 25 states with 331,800 subscribers at December 31, 1998

- Approximately 12% of the U.S. population can access one out of our points of presence through a local phone call.

We then had to meet with SEC attorneys and identify every possible risk we could think up and prioritize them in the order of potential impact. The grand list totaled twenty-two such possibilities. The reason we had to provide this in our offering is because we were obligated to inform potential buyers of how risky their investment in the IPO was.

I hated the pessimism that permeated this process. I'm an optimist by nature, and spending all that time concocting unlikely worst-case scenarios was not my strength and withered me emotionally. As it turned out, however, this exercise was great training for risk management and gave me real-world experience that I can apply to the numerous corporate and not-for-profit boards I serve on today.

Everyone worked very, very hard, and we got our 10-K filed with the SEC on December 30, 1998. What started as an eighteen-page business plan the previous February at the Chesapeake Bay had become a gargantuan 343-page SEC Form S-1 document. Sixty days after submission, the SEC got back to us with ninety-eight comments, not what you want to hear. Worse of all, they didn't like some of our accounting. I was close to livid with these federal bureaucrats and wanted to fight them tooth and nail because we had, after all, followed exactly what AOL did when they went public.

Remember my admonishment to "listen" in Chapter 7? Well, our attorneys advised us to suck it up and respond just as the SEC requested, including re-doing the financials, the time to market was much more important. "You'll probably lose your appeal anyway," one of our tax lawyers said.

Time was of the essence because the stock market was going wild—in a good way. Internet stocks were rallying like crazy. My plan called for the company to be named the United States Internet Providers.

At the last minute, though, our investment bankers recommended we change our name to OneMain.com, which would better communicate our corporate desire to "act local, think global." They had a point: we did have more than a few Main Street addresses in our 663 "points of presence" since every little town in America seems to have a Main Street. But the big reason we liked this name is become the "dot-com" in the title was a hot commodity on Wall Street. Don't ask me why, it just was.

As we put together a booklet for our road show, called a "red herring," we estimated our stock price could be in the $17-19 range, even though two months earlier we had figured that $10 per share would be our benchmark. At the conclusion of our thirty-city road show with groups of investors, retirement fund managers, and venture capitalists, we had 64,000,000 orders on the books for the 8,000,000 shares to be offered, a condition referred to as "oversubscribed."

That was a nice problem to have because when demand is greater than supply, the price goes up. We set the strike price at $22 per share on March 24, 1999, the day before issue. This meant the investment bankers had to go back to their buyers and see how many shares the investors wanted at the new higher price and then pro-rate the new desired share amounts, if we were still oversubscribed. In case you're wondering, that's why investment bankers make the big bucks.

We opened on NASDAQ at 11 a.m. on March 25, 1999, and began trading at $29 per share. Woo-hoo! The price kept climbing like a Saturn rocket. By 2:00 p.m., we had reached our apogee at $46 before settling closer to earth at $39 per share. Double woo-hoo.

We were the biggest gaining stock that day on Wall Street, and the CNBC pundits were all over the story. Next to marrying Doris and the birth of our three children, this was probably the most exhilarating day of my life. The ship had come in for a bunch of happy sailors who thought they were selling half their companies for $10 per share. Do the math in your head, and you can see that we got about *four times* that amount!

There's a dark side, though. I mentioned in the Introduction that around seventy-one individuals became millionaires or multi-millionaires that day. Later, in Chapter 15, I share both the beauty and the tragedy of that instant wealth. As the old saying goes, *Be careful what you wish for.*

Lucky Stars

As for Rod, Carlton, and myself, we shake our heads at what transpired. Boy, we were lucky because just one month later, AOL announced that they wouldn't hit their forecasted subscriber numbers for the 1st quarter of 1999. Their stock declined, and years later, we can state that AOL's downward trajectory was the beginning of the end for Wall Street's infatuation with anything Internet. As prices across the tech board continued their downward trend, this development ultimately led to the great 2001-02 technology bubble burst.

We were one of the fortunate and lucky players, and what a ride. We went from two employees to 1,500—many of them absolutely wonderful to work with—from one customer to 800,000, and changed headquarters three times in six years. What an incredible journey. Looking back—and this is craziest of all—it turns out that our highest market cap ever for our company . . . over $800 million . . . was at 2 p.m. on the day of our IPO.

As the market trended downward, AOL, EarthLink, and Microsoft Net were each trying desperately to grow subscribers.

AOL was way out in front in subscriber count, EarthLink was No. 2, and Microsoft Net was No. 3 but gaining on EarthLink. Suddenly, we were the fifth largest Internet company in the U.S. As our stock became more reasonably priced, three companies inquired about buying us. EarthLink wanted to add OneMain's 800,000 subscribers to their numbers to remain ahead of Microsoft, so they put in an offer to purchase our company.

When the offer came in, we initially said no, but the investment bankers on our board pointed out that the ISP market was changing rapidly and since we had a good offer from a reliable company, we needed to take it.

While we were mulling what to do, we received a certified letter from Cisco reducing our equipment line of credit, and then another certified letter from Bankers Trust reducing our acquisition line of credit even though we were making the numbers from which our credit lines were initially based upon. That's how skittish vendors were becoming as the air was seeping out of the tech bubble.

Ah, maybe we should take that offer on the table.

We decided to sell if we could get the right deal, so we entered into negotiations with EarthLink in May 2001. Five months later, all the i's were dotted and the t's were crossed and we closed in September 2001. *The Wall Street Journal*'s headline captured the Street's mindset: "EarthLink Strengthens No. 2 position with OneMain Acquisition."

So the four- to five-year "play" forecast by our investment banker was directionally right, except it happened a lot sooner—in two-and-a-half years.

Looking back as entrepreneurs, we had the fortitude to do what was required to survive. We took calculated risks. It's good we listened to our investment bankers because no one would give $315 million for 800,000 customers today.

As you think about our story, which admittedly is out of the ordinary, consider what happened to us as a great reminder of the rapid rate of change one has to manage today. The person who has written the book, so to speak, on change is John Paul Kotter, professor of leadership, emeritus, at the Harvard Business School. Known as a thought leader in the fields of business and leadership, Kotter is the author of *The Heart of Change*, which outlines his eight steps to managing change.

This would be a good place to review Kotter's eight-step process for change. They are as follows:

1. Create a sense of urgency.

Before you do anything else, you have to examine the market and competitive realities. Once you identify certain crisis points, you can discuss opportunities for advancement and creating a catalyst for change. Help others see the need for change through a bold, aspirational opportunity statement that communicates the importance of acting immediately.

2. Build a guiding coalition.

You need a team around you. Assemble a group with enough power to lead the change effort and then develop strategies for achieving that vision. A volunteer army needs a coalition of effective people—born of its own ranks—to guide it, coordinate it, and communicate its activities.

3. Form a strategic vision and initiatives.

Creating a vision for what happens next will help direct the change effort. Carefully and methodically develop strategies for achieving that vision. Clarify how the future will be different from the past and how you can make that future a reality through initiatives linked directly to the vision.

4. Enlist a volunteer army.

Make sure you use every channel and vehicle of communication possible to communicate the new vision and strategies.

In-person and face-to-face meetings are best. The guiding coalition should be teaching new behaviors and leading by example. Large-scale change can only occur when massive numbers of people rally around a common opportunity. They must be brought in and feel the urgency to drive change while moving in the same direction.

5. Enable action by removing barriers.

Start by removing obstacles to change. Next, change systems or structures that seriously undermine the vision. Be someone who encourages risk-taking and non-traditional ideas, activities, and actions. Removing barriers such as inefficient processes and hierarchies provides the freedom necessary to work across silos and generate real impact.

6. Generate short-term wins.

Start by planning for visible performance improvement, and when that happens, reward employees involved in these improvements. Wins are the molecules of results. They must be recognized, collected, and communicated—early and often—to track progress and energize your team.

7. Sustain acceleration.

When enacting change, you will have increased credibility to reshape systems, structures, and policies that don't fit your vision for the future. This is not the time to rest on your laurels. Press harder after the first successes. Be relentless with initiating change after change until the vision is a reality.

8. Institute change.

Develop channels to ensure leadership development and succession. Be sure to articulate the connections between the new behaviors and organizational success, making sure they continue until they become strong enough to replace old habits.

As Rod, Carlton, and I learned through our experience with SuperNet and OneMain.com, we live in a world where "business as usual" *is* change. Technological improvements, working to stay ahead of the competition, and new initiatives are aspects of today's modern business world that come together to drive ongoing changes to the way we work.

The lesson to be learned here: change is inevitable. In some cases, your little boat may need to transform into an ocean liner to take on the cargo opportunity in your path. If that should happen, be creative in collaborating with others to meet the challenge. If that means bringing in new partners to sustain acceleration, then do what you need to do to keep your entrepreneurial effort in full-speed-ahead mode.

ELEVEN

Watching the Shoreline

"One must always be prepared for riotous and endless waves of transformation."

—Elizabeth Gilbert, author of *Eat, Pray, Love*

"Discoveries are often made by not following instructions; by going off the main road; by trying the untried."

—Frank Tyger, editorial cartoonist and columnist
in the 1960s and 1970s

"New discoveries in science will continue to create a thousand new frontiers for those who would still adventure."

—Herbert Hoover, the 31st U.S. president from 1929-1933

As an entrepreneur, you are an innovator. You may also be a scientist. You might be an inventor. You could be a gifted computer programmer. Or you may be a talented individual who takes an idea and makes it better.

Today, the Internet provides an amazing platform for sharing information, for building collaborative partnerships, and for reaching niche customers worldwide. This relatively new world of collaboration and discoveries is the fun part of being an entrepreneur. If you like change, then entrepreneurship is a good place to be.

So how do you build a company that excels in innovation, allows the accidental to happen, and seeks to do the impossible? How do you organize a new business in a constantly changing business environment, manage today's challenges, and plan for tomorrow?

History shows how quickly the nature of business adjusts and reshapes itself. For example, consider the incredible technological changes that we've witnessed in the last thirty years—just one generation. Back in the mid-1980s, there was no Internet, no email, no voicemail, and no mobile devices. Personal computers were, for the first time, finding their way into corporate cubicles, but not every worker bee had a personal computer because they were expensive. Apple II computers generally cost $2,500 ($5,360 in today's dollars). The first Windows-based PCs were coming down in price, but you could figure on paying $1,500 ($3,200 in today's dollars) for a computer with a monitor, dual floppy disk drives, and a meager 64K of RAM memory. That was pricey for a lot of businesses and folks at home.

When people saw that they could type letters, memos, and manuscripts on a computer, edit their prose, and fix typing errors so easily—no more white-out, no more bulky electric type-writers—they wanted those incredible machines. When Microsoft software engineers came up with Excel spreadsheets and PowerPoint presentations, the business community sat up and took notice. When camera makers developed digital cameras that allowed photography enthusiasts and parents to snap incredible photos—as many as they wanted!—which could be easily viewed as well as stored on home computers, the consumer market blasted off into the stratosphere. These tech goodies fundamentally changed the way we do business and improved our lives. When the Internet came along in the 1990s, the way we interact with each other changed as well.

At the same time, prices on personal computers dropped so precipitously that just about everyone could afford one. Well, maybe not everyone since only 51 percent of U.S. households had a home computer in 2000, according to the U.S. Census Bureau, but that was a significant six-fold increase from 8.2 percent in 1984.

Once at the doorstep, Innovation didn't stop long to clean its feet in the 2000s. The rise of smartphones and development of tablet computers steered people away from their home computers because these new techno-gadgets were mobile and could be stowed in a messenger bag or purse when not in use. Meanwhile, laptop and desktop sales have contracted since they peaked in 2011 because people do more of their daily computing—email, web browsing, and social media—on their smartphones and tablets.

This lightning-round review of the computing world in the last three decades testifies to the fact that today's powerful computers enable one to process vast amounts of data with ease and accuracy that wasn't possible even a decade ago. Computers have become so ubiquitous that we can all agree with the old saying, "You can't live with computers and you can't live without them."

What this means for you, the entrepreneur, is that you have powerful tools to interpret data, streamline operations, and analyze trends at your fingertips. That said, you must stay on top of the technological side of your business. Bill Gates, the founder of Microsoft and the wealthiest man in the world with $86 billion in net worth, described business as a digital nervous system that learns to move at the speed of thought—like a living organism—in his book, *Business @ the Speed of Thought: Succeeding in the Digital Economy.* Gates stressed the need for entrepreneurs to view technology not as overhead but as a strategic asset that can help run businesses better today and transform the nature of business in the future.

If I can digress for a moment, I have an interesting personal story to tell about Bill Gates. Back in the late 1980s, when I was overseeing American Helix, our CD-manufacturing company owned by High Industries, one of the software engineers had an idea about putting the best sounds from various movies onto a CD-ROM. Actually, the idea was more complicated than that, but that was the gist of it.

Our software engineer suggested that we try to sell his idea to Microsoft. *Yeah, right.* But at the annual Microsoft convention in San Francisco, companies and vendors were invited to send in their pitch letters for new products or ideas and Microsoft would pick the Top 30. We got picked, which got us an audience with none other than Bill Gates himself.

In the tech world, that's like getting an audience with the Pope in Rome.

We were told to be at a certain conference room at the convention site at 5:45 p.m. I was a part of a team of four to see Gates. Of course, we arrived a good fifteen minutes early.

At 5:45, no Bill Gates. Fifteen minutes later, no Gates. How stupid we were to think that we would actually get to sit down with Bill Gates. We were just about to give up when, at 6:15, Bill Gates walked into the conference room.

"Hey, guys. Sorry about that. I ran into an old friend on the floor," he began.

Sure, Bill. No problem . . . .

What else are you going to say to Bill Gates?

He sat down and looked at our two-page proposal. What happened next was unbelievable. Let's say that we had one hundred issues to deal with in putting together this technology and had solved ninety-eight of them. Well, that son of a gun zeroed in on the two things we were still trying to figure out. I left the meeting shaking my head, saying, "This guy is a freaking genius."

We had spent $250,000 developing this technology. Another company had a somewhat similar package with ninety-nine of the one hundred issues figured out, so they beat us to the punch and became the industry standard. But what an experience spending thirty minutes in a conference room with Bill Gates—one of the highlights of my career.

Now, getting back to how you have to stay abreast of the latest technology . . . .

For example, take a look at the reduction of cycle times in manufacturing in the last ten years. These days, supply chains are designed for "just in time" delivery, eliminating warehousing costs and inventory holding expenses that have vexed entrepreneurs since the start of the Industrial Age. Steps in the process from sales to delivery can be integrated, resulting in more efficient operations. Information flows seamlessly from order entry to scheduling to manufacturing to inventory to delivery to the customer. Ingredients can be tracked in great detail to assure consumer safety or to pinpoint an exact recall, if required. Machinery utilization or "up time" can be optimized by integrated scheduling.

Or look at how underwriting happens today in the insurance industry, where ready access to credit scores—which take a tremendous amount of computing power and cooperation between banking firms—results in more accurate risk assessment and informed pricing. I urge you to use analytics to fine-tune your business decisions. Do everything you can to stay current on the computer side. Otherwise, you'll fall behind the competition, which could be the start of a downward spiral that proves to be difficult to control and nearly impossible to stop.

No entrepreneur wants to be put in that spot.

A Big Shift

This automation of information is shifting many jobs from redundant, often boring activity to more sophisticated positions or what I call "thinking jobs," where you contribute value by *analyzing* data as opposed to *entering* data. Finding ways to train and empower your employees to be thinking about ways to interpret data adds value to your company and is essential to the overall competitiveness and long-term success of your business.

This explosion of computer processing power and the impact of the Internet and social media is transforming business practices at an unbelievably rapid pace. Product life cycles are also becoming shorter in many industries due to the rapid pace of change and innovation. Many companies today employ SCADA—supervisory control and data acquisition—systems to run complex operations.

Twenty years ago, I spent a day accompanying one of our salespersons, who worked at our steel service center, during his rounds to various manufacturers of steel products. I'll never forget the back-to-back stops we made that day with two customers in a similar business. The first company was totally automated with CAD (computer-aided design) software on the design side and CAD-CAM (computer-aided design and computer-aided manufacturing) software to assist in all operations inside an extremely clean high-tech plant. During my tour, only a few white-coated employees were visible. Their job was to monitor a wall full of computer screens that provided information on the robots and machines churning out products.

The second company had a typical office environment with employees perched on stools next to drafting desks, using old style blueprints. Inside the plant, blue-collar welders cut designs into plates of sheet steel, and four men in blue overalls stood around a metal table, bent over a blueprint and discussing what to do next.

The contrast was incredible: a new computerized manufacturing plant versus the old way of doing business. In terms of commerce, one company was capital intensive, and the other was labor intensive. Which company do you think had the best chance of long-term survival?

Daryl Conner, in his book *Managing at the Speed of Change*, points out that it isn't enough to recognize that the way you do business will change. You have to be prepared to do far more and consciously build systems and employ teams that know how to make changes quickly, effectively, and economically with as little political fallout as possible. Learning *how* to change is as important as learning *what* to change, according to Conner, who's recognized for his consulting work on change management.

The rapid advance of technology and the corresponding shortening of product life cycles makes it critical that you mine your data to detect internal trends. It's imperative to stay abreast of external developments related to your business. If you don't, you could be left in the dust in a heartbeat.

Case in point: the BlackBerry.

The inventors of the BlackBerry, a Canadian company called Research in Motion (RIM), has met its Waterloo, which is ironic since the company is based in Waterloo, just outside of Toronto.

Once upon a time—like in the first half of the '00s—BlackBerry was the best-selling smartphone in the world. One out of every two smartphones was a BlackBerry because RIM was first to market with a cell phone that could send and receive emails, browse the Web, and display a digital calendar. Before the BlackBerry came on the scene, you had to carry around a cell phone and a Palm PDA (a personal digital assistant) if you wanted to do emails or surf the Internet when you were on the go.

I was one of those businessmen who got a BlackBerry when it first came out. In fact, our ISP was a BlackBerry dealer.

At the time, I thought my BlackBerry was a sensation. With an arched qwerty keyboard and sizable screen, I could send emails and messages effortlessly by tapping keys with both thumbs, a text-input method that *Forbes* magazine said was the best ever devised for a portable device. Fans like me were so enamored with their BlackBerrys that we called them "CrackBerrys." One of BlackBerry's biggest boosters was Barack Obama, when he famously said during his first presidential campaign, "I can't live without my BlackBerry."

And then the BlackBerry got steamrolled by innovation. The arrival of the iPhone and Android in 2007 and 2008, respectively, was like a champion mixed martial arts fighter climbing into the octagon with two worthy opponents. The two-against-one match up resulted in a BlackBerry beatdown: by 2012, just five and four years from the introduction of the iPhone and Android, BlackBerry was down from 50 percent of the smartphone market to just 6 percent. As people gravitated to using apps on the iPhone or checking out the sleekness and affordability of Android devices like the Samsung Galaxy—not to mention these smartphones' ability to take photos and make movies—sales of BlackBerrys dwindled to next-to-nothing. Down to less than 1 percent of the smartphone market, RIM threw in the towel in 2016.

The BlackBerry's story is an ominous sign of how quickly success can arrive and how fleeting success can be.

"We live in an era of constant disruption," said journalist Jacquie McNish, co-author of *Losing the Signal: The Untold Story Behind the Extraordinary Rise and Spectacular Fall of BlackBerry.* "No matter where you are, there's an algorithm or a new way of doing something that's more efficient, that challenges the old way of doing things."

The Other Side of the Coin—People

For all this talk about technology and the importance of staying on the cutting edge of technological revolution, I don't want to forget about people. They are, in fact, your most important asset.

Sure, technology is front-and-center in today's corporate world, but as the number of jobs that require cognitive skill increases, people are more important than ever. Daniel Pink, author of *Drive: The Surprising Truth About What Motivates Us*, says the rapid increase in "thought jobs" requires employees to be creative, solve problems, and think outside the box. You, as the entrepreneur, must pay close attention to how you can create a corporate culture that supports the creative process and problem solving. Remember that the people who work for you—your employees, your associates, or your team members—are your most important resource.

I've long valued people because of what was instilled in me at a young age by my parents, and it's a simple five-word phrase that's the cornerstone of this book: "Treat all persons with dignity."

My father mentored this attitude when I was growing up. An entrepreneur himself—he owned and operated a commercial flower-growing operation in Lancaster—I watched him always treat his suppliers and his customers with dignity. The woman buying $3 worth of carnations was treated the same as the wholesaler from Philadelphia who left a $100,000 purchase order on his desk. That's just the way Dad was.

I carried this attitude of treating people with dignity into my first job in the corporate world back in the 1970s. Victor F. Weaver, Inc., a food-processing firm in Lancaster County that produced chicken and turkey products, hired me to do corporate training and planning. Victor Weaver, the founder, was a true entrepreneur who opened a roadside stand on a two-lane highway between Lancaster and Philadelphia in 1937, selling broilers that were raised on the family farm. As business grew, Victor began buying from independent poultry farms. A year after opening his stand, Victor and his wife, Edith, purchased four acres of land in New Holland, Pennsylvania, that included a house, a shed, and a "chicken house," otherwise known as a processing plant.

Business grew rapidly in the 1940s and 1950s as word got around about Weaver's great-tasting chicken. In the 1960s, Weaver started producing frozen fried chicken and breaded chicken steak, which became a hit along the Eastern Seaboard all the way to Boston. When I started at Weaver, they had a clever ad campaign called "Step Aside, Southern Fried" that took on Colonel Sanders and his fried chicken cousins.

I liked working in a company where the Weaver family was closely involved in the day-to-day operations. Weaver didn't feel like a big corporation, which the company was at the time with annual sales of more than $50 million and 1,000 employees.

That's why I understood that when the Human Resources department got busy, they would tap me to do job interviews even though that wasn't part of my job description. I wanted to help out because one of the company's policies was that if someone showed up in person and filled out an application, he or she deserved the dignity of being interviewed right away. Since my office was next door to the personnel department, I was readily available to pitch in during busy times, as my schedule allowed.

Here was the situation: we had a lot of minority applicants who spoke broken English. Inside the Human Resources department, we had two personnel people who were bilingual, which was unusual back in the 1970s. Today, because of the immigration situation, a decent-sized company better have Spanish-speaking people in HR, but back then, that wasn't the norm. In fact, I remember the time when Armstrong Corp., a Fortune 500 company, sent five people from their HR department to check into the way we did things at Weaver. Afterward, the head of the delegation asked me, "How do you attract and keep these minorities? We try and try, and we can't do it. How do you do it?"

"How many bilingual people do you have in personnel?" I asked.

He gave me a shrug of the shoulders. "We don't have anyone who speaks Spanish," he said.

"Well, that's your reason," I said.

When I carried the motto "Treat all persons with dignity" into my work at Weaver, I reminded myself that meant *everyone*. I'll never forget one job applicant I interviewed. She had no high school education, no references. There was just one work experience on her application—picking apples in Kaufman's Orchard, which was a big orchard in Lancaster.

Her name was Mildred. She was white, very poor. Probably around thirty years old with a low IQ that became evident in the interview process. Of course, I treated her nicely and with respect, just as if she were a Rhodes Scholar.

"So, Mildred, you worked at the Kaufman Orchards," I began, using conversation to get Mildred talking about herself.

She got excited. "Yeah, yeah, every year, for about two or three weeks, I picked apples. I can climb a ladder. I can reach further than anyone else." Bless her heart, Mildred gave me a rather lengthy and glowing report on how well she could pick apples.

I wanted to hire her. She deserved a shot. I knew she could use the money.

We had an entry-level job in the plant that everyone hated, but it was a start, and from there you moved on to something else. Here's what the job entailed: when you slaughter a chicken, the carcass comes to the eviscerating area, where further processing is initiated. Often times, right where the neck and the breast meet, there are several feathers left on the skin; the machine that removed the feathers couldn't get the last few because that's the hardest place to get all the feathers off. Called pinfeathers, you don't want them on your whole fryers in the refrigerator case. That wouldn't make for good presentation and wasn't something American consumers were used to seeing.

The only solution to removing the last few pinfeathers was to have people on the line ready to pluck them off the neck. Some chickens had them, and some didn't. Nonetheless, I thought this entry-level job might be of interest to Mildred.

I walked her out to the plant. "I want to show you a job that we have," I said. After I introduced her to a supervisor, who showed her around the plant, they returned. The supervisor pulled me aside and said, "She's the most enthusiastic person I've ever seen."

"You want me to hire her?"

"Sure."

So I offered her the job. You'd think that picking pinfeathers off recently slaughtered chickens wouldn't be the most exciting job opportunity in the world, but Mildred absolutely loved being on the line. For openers, the position gave her the dignity of a job and a paycheck, which gave her some freedom in life. She proved to be a reliable employee.

Five years later, I was promoted to Vice President of Operations at Weaver. On many mornings, I'd drop by the plant early to say hello to the folks. I'd always start at the "vis line"—also known as the "kill line"—since the whole chicken processing plant runs off of that.

On the mornings when I arrived before the start of work, I'd

While I was still in my early thirties, I was named Vice President of Operations at Victor F. Weaver, Inc., a food processing firm in Lancaster County, Pennsylvania.

find Mildred in the break room, having a coffee. Every time she'd look at me and beam.

"Mr. Lefever, good morning, good morning!"

There were usually thirty other minorities there, half of whom didn't speak English so I couldn't talk to them much, but her engaging interaction with me made a relationship with all those other people possible. She was so loud and boisterous that her energy was contagious.

I found these interactions to be a perfect reminder that if you treat someone with dignity, then that person can blossom like a spring flower. Mildred was happy to have that job, proud of holding that job, and grateful to have money to spend. But she gave me back something precious in return as well. You see, I would have had a challenging time opening a conversation with some of the other minority persons in the early morning, but she opened the door for me.

Mildred stayed with Weaver a long time, and looking back, I'd say she was my best hire. Sure, she never rose to the executive suite or a managerial position, but she was an asset to our company and a vivid reminder of the importance of treating all persons with dignity.

The Unexpected Benefit of Community Service

When I started at Weaver in corporate training, I immediately joined the American Society for Training and Development, a trade association group that offered networking possibilities as well as do-good projects that helped the local community.

New Holland, a big company that built agricultural machinery and construction rigs in Lancaster County, had a full-time guy in employee training named Stan Canarius. He was older than me, and as I got to know him, he took me in as his mentor. Stan invited me to accompany him to meetings at the local Chamber of Commerce, Rotary Club, and United Way. I found this to be a way of broadening my base of contacts.

In my situation, I got involved the most with the United Way, a nonprofit organization that raises money and support for local schools, government agencies, worthwhile ministries, and neighborhood associations. I was asked to help United Way by calling on high-level executives and asking them if they wanted to support our direct-service programs and community-change efforts, which put me into personal contact with great business leaders like Dale High, the son of the founder of High Industries.

Dale and I developed a professional and personal relationship through our United Way involvement. We got to know each other and held the same values. We became friends, although I wouldn't say that we were close friends since Dale was several rungs up the economic ladder than me. But I never got the impression that he thought along those lines.

Eight years later, following promotions that put me in senior management at Weaver, I got a call from Dale, asking me to come over for lunch. "I have a few things I want to do and need to make a few hires, so I want to tap your brain."

We talked shop over a pleasant lunch. He outlined some things that were going on at High Industries and asked me if I knew anyone who'd be a good fit. I suggested five people from my circle. After writing down the names, he looked up.

"There's a rumor floating around the community, and I'm sure you've heard it too, that Weaver might be bought," he said.

I'd heard rumblings in the hallway, too. Weaver was a successful company, which made the firm ripe for a take-over bid. "Yes, you hear things," I conceded.

We both knew that it would be inappropriate of me to confirm or deny that Weaver was for sale. I didn't tell Dale that I was part of the team that was in the middle of the negotiations with Holly Farms, a billion-dollar company that was interested in buying Weaver. At the time, I had risen to Group Vice President of Operations and was on Weaver's board of directors.

As if reading my mind, Dale said, "I would never want to do anything to hurt the Weavers. Now, I'm not asking you to tell me whether it's true or not true, but if it's true that a sale is pending and you want to talk when the company is sold, let me know." Then Dale gave me a big wink.

What Dale and I both knew was that if a corporate suitor bought Weaver, they would have their management team run things; that's what usually happens when a bigger company purchases a smaller one. Sure enough, Holly Farms made an offer the Weaver family couldn't refuse. (Victor Weaver, seventy-five years old, had retired and would die within a year from cancer.)

That meant my days were likely numbered. When the Holly Farms deal went through, I contacted Dale.

"Great to hear from you, Allon. I've been holding a job for you," he said.

It wasn't just any job. In 1986, Dale brought me into the fold as Senior Manager with High Industries, which had an annual revenue north of $200 million. Dale also invited me to serve on his Executive Committee. In this position, over the next eleven years, I was part of a team that developed ten companies that contributed to rapid revenue growth and profitability for the parent company. I was given direct responsibilities for the operations of each company and selected presidents who reported to me. Over time, we sold five of these companies. Nonetheless, I oversaw annual revenues that grew to $400 million a year.

High Industries is where I was working when my son Rod came home from Dartmouth at Christmastime in 1992 and told about this thing called the "Internet," and the rest is history as they say. But as I look back at this pivotal time in my life, I know I wouldn't have had the experience to launch a successful entrepreneurial effort if I hadn't worked for Dale High at High Industries.

And the reason I got to know Dale High on such a close, personal level is because I volunteered to serve on United Way.

What to Ask

There are a couple of more things that I want to add about the "people side" to entrepreneurship. There's a good chance that if and when you hire employees, you will be doing the interviewing.

What are some things to look for when interviewing candidates?

I like to see people with a positive can-do attitude. In my hiring, I put a lot of importance on attitude and perspective, especially in a service industry like the hotel business since I own a Hampton Inn.

To help me unearth people's attitude about life, I often ask them to tell me a story about something they did that they found rewarding. I don't want to hear about an award they received or about some honor or degree they earned. I'm hoping to hear about something that involved them helping other people. It could be a time they volunteered to help out at a homeless shelter during the Thanksgiving holiday or the time they joined their church on a missions trip to Costa Rica.

Another question I like to ask is this: "Tell me about a team project that you have been involved in, or tell me something you did at school that was team-oriented."

I'm looking to see if they've worked in a team setting before. Some will talk about playing on a sports team, and that can be a good thing since that means they learned to work with others on a common goal as well as push themselves to the limit. At the same time, though, it's surprising how many haven't been in a team setting. A lot of young people, especially those consumed by technology, are used to leading singular lives.

Another thing I like to see in an interview is eye contact. If you sit across a table from someone who doesn't look back at you or is shy, that could mean he or she is an introvert. That's not necessarily a bad thing, but if you're hiring a front desk person for a hotel, you probably want a bubbly extravert who likes greeting weary travelers as they set their bags down and commence the hotel check-in.

One thing I'm careful with is that I don't separate too much the extravert from the introvert. It's easy for me to hire extraverts because they come across as go-getters, but some introverts are very good at interacting with people in a polite and professional manner.

Another thing I look for is curiosity. I try to sense if they are relentlessly inquisitive about how things work and what their job would be like. Are they asking me questions about the job? Are they interested in what our company is trying to do? Are they naturally curious individuals?

I like to see a sense of curiosity and an innate desire to learn about new things. People who are curious are better problem-solvers because they are looking for answers, and these are the type of people you want to hire for your "thought jobs."

And now, I want to ask you an interview question: What type of leader are you? You may or may not choose to answer, but are you more of an authoritarian, top-down type of leader, or are you a participatory leader, where decisions are made with the most feasible amount of participation possible from those who are affected by the decisions?

I've always been a huge fan of participatory leadership as opposed to authoritarian/top-down, but I've had to work at that because my personality can be aggressive. Maybe that's why I shot up the ladder at Weaver pretty fast, but I got a rude awakening of how an assertive management style can impact others when I was asked to participate in a 360° multi-rater feedback tool in which I, as the supervisor, received performance feedback from eight people who worked directly under me.

They answered survey questions on a rating scale and provided written comments covering a broad range of workplace competencies. The feedback was done confidentially and anonymously. I, as the person receiving feedback, also filled out a self-rating survey that included the same survey questions that the eight others received in their forms.

I was certainly interested in what the results would be since 360° feedback shows you how you rated yourself and how the others saw you as a group. Well, as Steve Harvey, the host of the *Family Feud* game show would say, "And the survey said . . . ."

And the survey said I rated myself as an 8 (on a scale of 1-10, 10 being best) as an effective leader. My eight employees, however, rated me as a 6.

Ooh, I thought I was better than that. Maybe I'm being perceived differently than what I perceive myself.

The written comments can be summarized in one short sentence: *He is intimidating.* This surprised me because I thought I was really good at involving people. I would try to run meetings and not act like I had all the answers but ask people what they thought. I thought I was good at that, but the 360° feedback reported that I came across as intimidating.

I was young when I received this feedback—probably thirty years of age. The feedback caused me to do some soul-searching. I thought about how I had reached this point. For one thing, I was managing supervisors who were older than me. I was in a company that didn't have a lot of highly educated people. I had a master's degree in economics and had been in a Ph.D. program, so I was one of the more educated persons.

In fact, the reason why I went up the ladder so fast in the early 1970s is because the Soviet Union started buying corn because of massive crop failures. Corn had been $2 a bushel forever, but with Russians buying up every bushel they could, the price doubled to $4 a bushel. Weaver, which raised chickens for slaughter, had a lot of money tied up in feed costs, and chickens ate a lot of corn. We needed a hedging strategy because our director of purchasing got on the wrong side of the corn futures market.

I was asked by the vice president of Purchasing to come up with hedging strategy because portfolio strategy was part of my master's program. I had never written a commodity-hedging program, however, but since I knew more than anyone in the company, I was given the task.

Meanwhile, we were hemorrhaging money because we hadn't locked in future commodity purchases of corn. The VP of Purchasing's mistakes provided an opportunity for me to develop a more sophisticated approach to purchasing, which made me a hero of sorts within Weaver. Long story short, but a vice president over the broiler grow-out operations and purchasing was dismissed, and I was asked to temporarily oversee that important area until senior management figured out what they were going to do. Well, temporary became permanent. After that break, I zoomed several steps up the ladder at a young age and took on quite a lot of responsibility.

Victor Weaver, the founder of the company, was retiring, and he could have chosen from among five or six guys who were mostly closer to his age to succeed him, but he chose his son, Dale, to take over. Dale Weaver is the one who tapped me as a senior executive, which meant I was the first younger guy on his team, so to speak.

Over the next couple of years, as older guys retired, I was given additional executive management responsibilities. Remember, I wasn't even thirty years old, but I had long-time managers in their forties and fifties reporting to me.

And then I got viewed as intimidating in the 360° feedback—and rightly so. Hearing that in the early stages of my career was probably the best thing that could have happened to me. Why? Because I had to stop and assess what it meant. I knew I would have to work hard not to come across as intimidating.

I was fortunate to hear about a concept called "servant leadership," which was starting to gain traction in the business world. Robert K. Greenleaf, who worked forty years for AT&T in management development, had released a book called *The Servant as Leader* in 1970 in which he coined the phrase *servant leadership*. He asserted that the servant-leader puts the needs of others first and helps those around him (or her) develop and perform as highly as possibly.

I reminded myself that other people *can* make a decision. In meetings with those who reported to me, I made sure the team processed alternatives. I looked for opportunities to go around the conference table and ask, "What do you think?"

People noticed, and my 360° feedback got better. After Weaver sold and I went to work at High Industries, I was put in charge of all the strategic planning for their holding companies. When I worked with the senior management teams, I made sure I asked for their recommendations but I was also quick to inquire, "What would be an alternative strategic plan?" Everyone felt involved, and employee morale was high.

You are the captain of your ship. But be open to feedback. In fact, find ways to assess how you are doing. If you find a trait that needs improvement, work on it.

The lesson to be learned here: The world is changing more rapidly than ever before, given the explosion in technology. Stay abreast of technology, build systems and teams that can respond quickly and accurately to these winds of change, seek their input, guard against coming across as intimidating, and constantly watch the shoreline for clues of where your entrepreneurial ship is heading.

TWELVE

Loading the Cargo

"The first man gets the oyster; the second man gets the shell."
—Andrew Carnegie, 19th century American industrialist

"Hard work beats talent when talent doesn't work hard."
—Tim Tebow, former NFL quarterback
and major-league baseball hopeful

Given all the hard work you've done to launch your business, along with building an infrastructure to handle product or make widgets or warehouse inventory, you have to be ready to ramp up if your entrepreneurial effort takes off.

This may mean bringing on more capacity, in the form of specialized human resource talent, or increasing your production capacity. Running wide open can be both exhilarating as well as stressful. The more you're prepared for a surge in demand, the less stressful this phase will be.

Many products have a life cycle that starts somewhat slowly, and then as they gain popularity, they enter a rapid growth stage before leveling off and eventually giving way to a better or less expensive product.

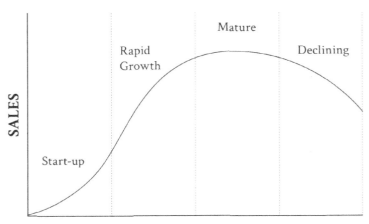

TYPICAL PRODUCT LIFE CYCLE

Figuring out what products will "trend" can be as fickle as figuring out the next viral video to hit it big. I remember back in the mid-1970s when I saw a *Newsweek* story about the Pet Rock. Apparently, an out-of-work copywriter named Gary Dahl heard his friends complaining about taking care of their dogs and cats, so he came up with the perfect "pet"—a rock.

This is when Dahl turned into an entrepreneur. He wrote a hilarious, tongue-in-cheek thirty-two-page manual on the caring, feeding, and house training of Pet Rocks and designed a cardboard carrying case, complete with air holes, that contained a smooth stone from Mexico's Rosarito Beach set on a bed of straw. Dahl paid one cent for each small stone and sold his Pet Rocks for $3.95 each. Nice markup.

The entire venture was a total joke and an easy target for late-night comics like Johnny Carson, which only fueled even more sales. Turns out Dahl had the last laugh: he sold 1.5 million boxes of Pet Rocks in six months and became an overnight millionaire.

You never know what will catch the public's fancy. I would have never thought that bitter-tasting kale, which is an incredible nutritional powerhouse of vitamins, minerals, and disease-fighting antioxidants, would be embraced by the American palate in recent years, but today you can buy all sorts of kale chips, kale popsicles, and kale tomato sauce. Recent trending products that are killing it have been matcha tea, coffee scrubs, coconut oil-based products, print-on-demand apparel, beard oil, drones, adult coloring books (very big), and wooden glasses (not so big).

Will your product satisfy a big itch? Or is it more than a novelty item like the Pet Rock? If you think your product will be a winner—and people you trust are encouraging you to go for it—then you better get ready for fast sales. That means forecasting more production and maintaining fulfillment so that you don't get into a backlog situation. Design ways to be flexible in your production output, staying one step ahead of sales, but be careful about building up excess inventory since that can lock up loads of capital.

In most service industries, you're not dealing with as steep a growth curve nor as rapid a decline as selling products. Even though service businesses are somewhat less impacted by technology, be aware that service innovations are occurring all the time. We're starting to see that in the fast food world where touch-screen kiosks are taking orders instead of a real live human being. I don't personally favor touch screens happening at front desks of hotels like mine, but who knows what the future will bring?

What a lot of service industries are facing is a fluctuating volume of service requirements during peak periods. If you're opening a restaurant, then you're aware of a big spike over lunchtime with customers on a tight schedule, so the kitchen better be ready and service needs to be snappy. Then there's a slow period from

2-5 p.m., but things pick-up as people come in for dinner—and everyone needs to be on their A game again.

Whatever your entrepreneurial business is, study the patterns. Design processes that enable fluctuation in service capability. It may mean preparing some items in advance, it may mean staffing for peaks, or it may mean cross-training persons to provide more flexibility. Whatever fits your business, put that plan in motion.

At the Hampton Inn, summers are our peak season, so I definitely need two persons on the front desk at all times. In the slow season, I may only need that second person from 5-9 p.m. when check-ins peak for the evening. Or, in the breakfast area, one breakfast hostess is usually adequate, but if we have a fifty-passenger bus staying at the hotel that is planning to leave at 8 a.m., then I know that group will descend upon our breakfast area between 7 and 7:15.

It doesn't make sense to bring in a second breakfast hostess for a morning shift just to cover a forty-five-minute rush, so I've cross-trained other employees to help out in that area for an hour or so and then return to their "regular job." Most employees like a break from the routine and feel like they are "pitching in" when asked to help out.

Learning to know your business, its trends, and how they impact your service level is often the difference between a good service level and a great service level. And in the service industry, outstanding service brings repeat business. Just look at how Chick-fil-A is crushing it when compared to chicken chain restaurants, thanks to its reputation for good service.

Chick-fil-A's average sales per restaurant are around $3 million annually, while KFC, its main competitor, comes in around $900,000. What's even more amazing about this statistic is that

Chick-fil-A is closed on Sundays but outperforms all of its competitors, which open their doors seven days a week! Chick-fil-A's founder, Truett Cathy, a devout Southern Baptist, decided when he opened his first restaurant in Hapeville, Georgia, back in 1946, that his most important "company value" would be closing on Sundays—the Sabbath. Cathy believed that all of his restaurant operators and employees should have an opportunity to rest, spend time with family and friends, and go to church if they choose to do so. Today, there are over 2,000 locations, so you have to say this key decision is part of Chick-fil-A's recipe for success.

The chicken-producing company that I worked for—Weaver—had a similar corporate policy about working on Sundays. Victor Weaver, the founder, was a religious man who felt Sunday should be set aside as a day of rest and going to church with your family—so working on Sunday was strictly forbidden.

Well, we had a fleet of eighty or ninety trucks that delivered fresh chickens and frozen fried chicken up and down the East Coast. They had to be back at the plant with their rigs by Saturday at midnight.

Victor was strict about this policy, so strict that we had scores of night truckers showing up at midnight on *Sunday night* so that they could begin driving after 12 a.m. and be in Baltimore and New York by the dawn's early light.

Weaver wasn't a vendor for Chick-fil-A, but I always knew that Victor Weaver appreciated their Sabbath stance. I'd say this corporate value of no work on Sunday contributed to their success.

Where the rubber meets the road in the restaurant world is customer service. As I've alluded to, Chick-fil-A consistently ranks first in restaurant customer-service surveys, with customers raving about the restaurants' cleanliness, their fast, convenient service, and their hardworking, polite employees. A noteworthy thumbs up comes from readers of *Consumer Reports*, which ranked Chick-fil-A as having the best service of any fast food restaurant chain in the country. That's the way you build customer loyalty, one customer at a time.

Chick-fil-A believes its service is consistently excellent because the company invests more in employee training than other fast food chains. In your situation, whether you're producing products or are in the service industry, it's critical to bring on a specialist in customer service training. We did this at the Hampton Inn when we found a female trainer who was incredible at helping us role-play what outstanding service looked like with different customer types, from the tired and weary to the nasty.

In you're in the service industry, observe and survey your customers regularly to understand what they value about your service and what can be improved. You can try tweaking your service to discover new ideas resonate with your customer. For example, we started asking younger children—during the Hampton Inn check-in process—to pick a "welcome prize" out of a box (such as a small toy or coloring book). We also added soymilk as an option at breakfast.

Watch what your competition is doing so that you can learn from their endeavors, but don't forget to pay close attention to the needs of your employees. When you expect them to always treat the customer well, they will certainly perform better if you also always treat them well. Be liberal with praise. Implement recognition and reward programs for outstanding customer service. Promote a fun-to-be-at-work atmosphere. Build camaraderie and give your employees a sense of belonging. Pizza parties are fun, but monetary rewards or a "trip of your choice" at the fifth and tenth anniversary of employment go a long way with your employees.

Pay special attention to worker safety because providing a safe working environment is part of every company with a positive and caring culture. An emphasis on employee and guest safety goes right to the bottom line. When you establish safety and health management systems, you can reduce injury and illness costs by 20 to 40 percent. It can get *expensive* when you have a worker's comp situation come up and OSHA (Occupational Safety & Health Administration) and state work inspectors show up. I'm happy to report that in 2016, we had 34,000 guests at our hotel and not a single safety incident. We celebrated that milestone with a pizza party for all employees.

Don't forget that the tendency for accidents is greater when everyone is running at full speed and haven't been adequately trained to do their job.

As you add employees, obtaining a good track record in worker safety will help you keep insurance premiums for workers comp as low as possible. If you reach a certain size in terms of employees, it might be cost-effective to add a full-time specialist who focuses on enhancing safety for both employees, customers, and even products.

You probably don't want to hear this, but regulatory requirements will expand as your business grows in size. This is what business is like in America today, so be prepared for some frustrating moments, especially in the area of providing health care for your employees, given the current political climate. Keeping on top of the health insurance equation will be an ongoing responsibility.

Growing and Growing

If and when you grow your company to a certain size, it may be advantageous to acquire other companies and fold them into your business. You may find opportunity in combining forces with a strategic partner, but an acquisition can be a good way to add output capacity, expand into new geography, add new products, or simply to take advantage of economies of scale.

Doing your research or "due diligence" is a must, from the simplest deal to the most complicated acquisition. When considering a merger or an acquisition, evaluate the culture fit. I have seen too many M&A (merger and acquisition) failures spring forth from a clash of cultures. One that comes quickly to mind was when Chrysler and Daimler-Benz—the German makers of Mercedes cars—agreed to a $36 billion merger in 1999. The auto press called it a "merger of equals."

The idea was that Chrysler would use Daimler parts, components, and even vehicle designs to sharply reduce costs on the assembly line. Here's where the clash of cultures raised its head: Daimler's Mercedes-Benz division, a brand synonymous with luxury, didn't want to share its parts or anything else in their cars with a mass-market partner like Chrysler. I guess it wasn't a merger of equals after all.

It took nine years of mistrust between the German side—with a company culture that was conservative, efficient and safe—and their American counterparts—with a company culture that was daring and diverse—to agree that DaimlerChrysler wasn't working. Their partnership was dissolved in 2007 for a mere $7.6 billion. As they say in the M&A field, "Ouch."

We live in a global economy, so it behooves you to pay attention to the impact of culture on your company. I realize that M&A are part of corporate strategies these days and are seen as a way to combine different companies so that a business can grow rapidly in its space or perhaps in a new country. But they aren't a panacea.

On the flip side of automotive mergers, one that worked was when TATA, an India-based group comprising over one hundred companies with operations in more than one hundred countries across six continents, merged with Jaguar Land Rover in 2008. Basically what you had was managers from India interacting with managers from Great Britain, which seems like a situation ripe for conflict, but TATA didn't leave the current managers on their own.

What TATA's managers did was walk a tricky line by offering to help only when help was needed while continuing to challenge the executive team at Jaguar Land Rover to do better. Instead of imposing a foreign culture like Daimler-Benz did with Chrysler, TATA respected the existing culture that was in place with the iconic British automakers. Today, TATA Jaguar Land Rover is making money and employing 35,000 people worldwide.

There has been a blizzard of mergers in my industry—hotels—in the last few years, mirroring what's been happening with the airlines (Delta merging with Northwest, United with Continental, and American with US Airways). These days, nearly half of the 53,400 hotels worldwide belong to one of the six hotel giants—Marriott, Hilton Worldwide, Intercontinental, Wyndham Worldwide, Choice Hotels, and Best Western Hotels & Resorts.

Mergers are happening all the time. In 2015, France's AccorHotels purchased the luxury Fairmont, Raffles, and Swissotel brands; Intercontinental Hotels acquired Kimpton, Marriott purchased Delta Hotels and followed that up a year later with a takeover of Starwood Hotels in 2016, creating a mammoth company with 5,800 hotels in one hundred countries.

I understand that mergers have a hit-or-miss quality to them—or become total flops. The $350 billion merger between AOL and

Time Warner back in 2001 is a textbook case of how the brightest minds in technology and media collaborated in a deal that many regard today as a colossal mistake. The merger was supposed to give Time Warner the ability to reach a new online audience, and in return, AOL received access to Time Warner's cable systems that, at the time, reached 40 percent of U.S. online subscribers.

The integration of the two companies was a total bust. The "corporate culture" between them turned out to be a Grand Canyon-sized gulf in which the executives at the two gigantic companies seemed to resent each other. Feuds developed over who would take the top leadership positions. Everyone was out to protect his or her turf.

Getting everyone on the same page is far easier said than done, of course. A well-thought-through Vision Statement is paramount, followed by an Annual Plan that provides a roadmap of where the newly merged company will go. When mergers go south, it's often because executives have made promises that they could not or would not keep. When promises are broken, word gets around quickly. Credibility evaporates, and morale of the merged company is affected negatively.

I was part of a roll-up in the supplies industry where we initially told the companies we acquired that they would be able to keep their IT systems. As we grew and got larger with more consolidated companies, it became obvious we had to build a common IT system that worked for everybody. You'd think that would be obvious to everyone, as it was to our side, but the previous owners—who were now our employees—felt they had been lied to. We tried to explain and show them how the situation had changed, but they continued to struggle with the conversions from their home-bred IT systems to ours as their familiar system was "retired."

Had we thought through the long-term IT consequences up front, we would have framed things differently with the company we were acquiring and proceeded with the merger anyway. Everyone would have entered the union with an expectation that a new IT system was a possibility. Instead, we were accused of breaking our promise to allow them to continue using their IT system, which prompted a gnashing of teeth.

No matter how smooth it looks on paper, integrating an acquired company can be challenging. New work teams, unfamiliar systems, and different procedures must be thoughtfully consolidated with care. If you don't smooth out ruffled feathers, you can expect to lose talent from those working in the acquired company. Open and consistent communication is essential to mitigating the natural concerns surrounding an acquisition.

Slow and Steady Is Sometimes Better

While getting the integration done in a timely manner is important, be careful not to implement too many changes all at once.

One of the public companies where I was a board member literally blew apart good managerial talent when an investment banking firm brought in too many of its own "smart" MBAs in an attempt to implement twelve strategic initiatives simultaneously. The result was chaos that totally overwhelmed the system, and we lost many capable, experienced managers to rival companies. Not good! I filed away that experience and applied what I learned correctly when SuperNet was actively acquiring companies in preparation for taking the company public.

Capital requirements for acquisitions need to be in place, and within reason. Do not make the mistake of overleveraging the company beyond what it can handle. Acquisition integration often takes more time, and you can expect to dole out more money than expected. Or, in some cases, customers of the acquired company can be lost, bringing less return than expected. Be sure to study the company carefully, agree upon an integration plan, and execute with care.

The lesson to be learned here: Be prepared to take advantage of openings in your market when the opportunity presents itself. Consider acquisitions and mergers if it makes business sense, but do intensive due diligence and have adequate financing.

THIRTEEN

Bringing in the Catch

"Don't judge each day by the harvest you reap but by the seeds you plant."

—Robert Louis Stevenson, Scottish novelist and poet

"For everything there is a season, a time for every activity under heaven. A time to be born and a time to die. A time to plant and a time to harvest."

—Ecclesiastes 3:1-2 (NLT)

At some point in your journey, there is a time to harvest—to reap what you have sewn. After investing so much of your time, your talent, and your money in your entrepreneurial business or service, there will come a time when you think it's appropriate or necessary to get a return on your investment. In other words, it will be harvest time.

Harvesting can take many forms. You can choose an exit strategy that grooms your children to take over when you're ready to go read a book on the beach somewhere. You can sell off part of the company but still retain control by keeping more than 50 percent of the action. You can sell off more than 50 percent of the company and take a back seat but still have a voice on the board. Or you can sell your company outright and move on while the going is good—or before it's too late.

Timing is everything, right? If we had waited three to six months to sell SuperNet for $308 million, we could have lost over $100 million. We had a feeling that it was the right time to cash out, and I have a hundred million reasons why I'm glad we did.

Some choose not to sell because they want to pass the business on to the next generation or to a loyal and competent management team. Having been through a number of harvest situations and having consulted many others, I will share a few observations.

First is that many small business owners don't have an exit strategy for their businesses when they retire or in the event of their death. I can't say I'm terribly surprised. Many entrepreneurs are so focused on surviving and growing their business that they don't have time to think about a succession plan or an exit strategy.

At the minimum, you need to choose a successor in case you get struck by a car while in a crosswalk. Tomorrow is never a guarantee, so have a successor waiting in the wings just in case the unexpected happens. Perhaps this will give you some peace of mind knowing that your life's achievement is in good hands.

But enough of these macabre thoughts. Moving forward, I want to imprint this point upon your memory right now: you usually only get one chance to transfer the business in some form, so think through what you want to do. Once you sell your company to an outside firm, the chances of ever getting it back are slim to none.

If you are blessed to own a family business, and you wish to pass it on to the next generation, I strongly urge you to explore every possibility to do just that. There's no reason why a good family business can't be passed on to the next generation—and future ones as well. Besides, what a great legacy to leave behind. The last time I checked, a Brinks truck doesn't follow a hearse.

Passing along the family business doesn't suddenly happen overnight. There should be many years of preparation as your children grow up. You want to give them the advantage of watching you and learning many aspects of the business, almost through osmosis. That's how my father and grandfather did when I grew up. They had a large greenhouse operation that grew flowers for the commercial market, among other things they did.

I like it when sons and daughters start at the entry-level jobs and work their way up. We used to call it "working in the mail room" when I started in the corporate world—a place where incoming U.S. Postal mail was sorted for delivery within the company. Now that "mail rooms" aren't very busy these days, I suppose the entry-level jobs are something like "front desk clerk" or "sales assistant," but it doesn't matter where they start. It's where they finish, and you want them to grow in your company. Keep in mind that as your children advance, they will get to know your employees, observe how the business operates, learn who your customers are, and gain valuable experience.

Establishing a pathway, policies, and procedures for the next generation is advisable. Some families form "family councils," where the next generation is exposed to various aspects of the business and hear their elders enunciate their expectations for the business. Some parents require a college education while some require working for a period of time at a firm other than the family business so they can gain maturity and experience. I have seen policies that require a promotion in another job. This early involvement helps train the next generation about the responsibilities of being a good employee.

Succession planning needs to be done for both management transition and ownership transition. The management transition involves planning for the roles to be played by the incoming generation. Care needs to be taken for the role and feelings of the current management team as no one likes to be elbowed out of the way or told they're history. You should have a worthwhile discussion about the long-term management roles for those who stay on. Ask your existing managers how they can assist in the development of future management so that when they leave, the company will not lose a step.

Evaluating various methods of ownership transfer is important. Three of the most common ways to transfer a business is through gifting ownership, selling ownership, or transferring ownership through a stock bonus. Each has potentially huge tax implications, which is why you should seek out accountants and legal professionals when you enter this stage.

I prefer to work with both the out-going generation and the in-coming generation, which helps me understand everyone's wishes. In the past, I would start with the out-going generation to determine their thinking and get an understanding of their preferred approach and timing. Then I would take the knowledge I gained from those discussions to begin working with the incoming generation.

I have changed my thinking over the years, however, and it's partly because the outgoing generation is often reluctant to breech the subject of succession because they don't want to risk family tensions or be accused of showing favoritism—situations that they would rather not face.

What I do now is get permission from the outgoing generation to enter into discussion and development of a framework that the incoming generation is ready to propose. Then I meet with the outgoing generation to share where their offspring is thinking.

Sounds simple, but there are three main advantages to this approach:

1. The parents are often relieved that they haven't had to make difficult calls.

2. The incoming generation has ownership and commitment in the plan.

3. Having the basic framework for the future management and ownership in place *before* the negotiations begin (for price, timing, etc.) ensures a smoother transformation.

If the outgoing generation needs money to live on during retirement, this makes succession of the ownership more workable at a fair price, enabling the business to meet cash flow and survive. This can be in the form of a long-term note, giving the incoming generation sufficient time for cash flow from the business to pay off the note.

The outgoing generation then has an interest in supporting the ongoing success of the new arrangements and the well-being of the business.

Another Approach

In the event there is no interest or competency or ability of the next generation to take over the family business, you may want to explore the advantages of forming an ESOP (Employee Stock Ownership Plan) as a tax-efficient way for you to transition the business to your employees. Again, find a good ESOP accountant and legal team as there are distinct rules on how to go about forming an ESOP.

Of course, an outright sale to a buyer outside the family or to your employees is always an option. If you sell to an outside party, I would urge you to get as much as you can upfront since cash is always king. Study the pros and cons of an asset sale as compared to a stock sale. In some cases, there will be tax advantages in a stock swap sale, but you are also taking on the risk of the acquiring party.

I have seen owners do a stock exchange for the value of their company because they hoped to save taxes only to lose a major portion of their value when the stock of the acquiring company declined unexpectedly. Again, an important reason to get as much cash on the sale as possible.

Harvest time is never a good time to be rushed. Carefully assess your options. Do careful due diligence if you are combining with another company.

Think ahead on what you plan to do from the resulting harvest. How much money do you need to live on? What are your lifestyle needs? What do you want to give to your church or favorite charities? Estate planning needs to be integrated into the ownership planning.

Good succession planning will enhance your chances of a successful transition of ownership, the ongoing success of your business, and be an important aspect of your legacy.

Sometimes the best-laid plans do not work for you. I saw an example of a family with two sons and a daughter, all of whom wanted to stay in the business as owners and managers. They worked out an elaborate multiyear plan in which the father would become chairman of the board, the oldest son would be president for five years, at which time the father would totally retire and the first son would become chairman of the board and the second son would then become president. Five years after that, No. 1 son would step aside as chairman of the board, taking a regular seat, and the No. 2 son would become the new chairman of the board. Then the daughter would become president of the company.

All signed off on the agreement, and it looked perfect on paper. Sadly, and to some surprise, within a year there were major disagreements on strategy, and the plan completely fell apart. To make a long and difficult story short, the daughter found a way to buy out her brothers and became the sole owner, president, and CEO of the business.

This sounds very much like what happened to Jeanie Buss, who squabbled with her brothers, Jim and Johnny, about who would take control of the Los Angeles Lakers NBA franchise following the death of their father, Jerry Buss, in 2012. Having six Buss children as co-owners of 66 percent of the Lakers complicated matters; no one knew who was in charge. Jeanie and Jim, who'd been working in some capacity for the Lakers for many years, were at loggerheads on who would run the team. There were restraining orders and court actions and a lot of filed motions, but in the end, Jeanie hammered out an agreement with Jim and Johnny to wrest control and be on the board of directors. The media called Jim and Johnny's attempt to take over the Lakers a "failed coup."

The lesson to be learned here: Harvest time represents the culmination of all your hard work and often your career, along with all the many relationships you formed over the years. But don't forget that nearly all the time, you only get one chance at this important decision, so proceed with caution, care, and love.

FOURTEEN

Time to Unload

"What you get by achieving your goals is not as important as what you become by achieving your goals."

—Zig Ziglar, motivational speaker

"All men seek one goal: success or happiness. The only way to achieve true success is to express yourself completely in service to society. First, have a definite, clear, practical ideal—a goal, an objective. Second, have the necessary means to achieve your ends— wisdom, money, materials and methods. Third, adjust all your means to that end."

—Aristotle, ancient Greek philosopher

Whether you wax as philosophical as the great Aristotle or not, his point is that during this journey called life, it's good to have a practical goal, the means to achieve it, and the wherewithal to "just do it," as the Nike slogan has told us for years.

And that's my encouragement to you—to become an entrepreneur who's driven by an idea that can help make this world a better place.

But now I want you to project yourself into the future—a time when you've passed along the day-to-day operations to the next generation or sold your business because the time was right, or the offer was too good to pass up, or you've reached the age where you want to slow down. In other words, you're ready for the fourth quarter of life, knowing that you've fulfilled your dream.

Have you thought about how you will transition from today's hectic entrepreneurial pace? What is it that you want to do in the remaining days that God has given you?

You can go off and do whatever you most enjoy—spending time with the family and grandkids, or join a country club and play a lot of golf, or travel to visit interesting cultures or take in magnificent scenery. But there's one more thing I want you to consider, and that would be looking for ways to use your entrepreneurial skills to make this a better world. You start by becoming involved in wonderful causes that appeal to your values and sense of community.

I will share my involvement with Goshen College and Eastern Mennonite University, non-profit organizations like Habitat for Humanity, and serving on non-profits boards of directors in greater detail in my final chapter. I can assure you that the satisfaction that I've gained is tremendous. There's truth in Jesus' words when He said, "It is more blessed to give than to receive" (Acts 20:35, NIV).

When and if there comes a time when you step away from your entrepreneurial business, it's important to remind yourself to let go of the past as quickly as you can. This is easier said than done. If your family is working alongside you when you step away, be present and available if asked for advice but don't continue to call the shots. The next generation will not always do things the way you did, or the way you would, but it is now their business. Let them make changes, try new ideas, and even fail at some things. They will learn from their mistakes just as you did in your start-up.

If you have sold your business to investors outside the family and no longer have any stake in the company, I think it's wise to completely remove yourself from the business. This is when I counsel to move on to other causes where you can make a meaningful contribution.

There are thousands of excellent non-government organizations, or NGOs, as well as beneficial charities that need worthy volunteers such as you to serve on committees or boards of directors. I have been involved in two continuing care retirement communities, or CCRCs, which need help in keeping costs under control so the elderly who live there—many on limited, fixed incomes—can afford to continue to live there. Some run out of money and need benevolent care, which is a challenge.

Or you may prefer to look into opportunities for service with worldwide organizations that provide helpful development programs to persons in many developing countries. These opportunities open up new exciting ways for continuing to learn and appreciate other cultures.

Different Transitions

I once consulted a company where the father, in his late sixties, was ready to enjoy life more as well as serve others. He continued to hold on to 99 percent of the business, however, even though his capable son was running the show. As you can surmise, the father just did not want to let go, especially of his ownership.

The son, in his forties, was increasingly frustrated by the reality that he was managing the business—as well as responsibility for its success—but 99 percent of the profits went straight into his father's pocket. In his mind he was thinking, *Why should I bust my hump when I'm nothing more than a salaried employee?*

He knew he had job skills and the right experience to go off on his own venture, and he was thinking about taking that course of action. When things got to that point, the father called me in to help them get through the major bump in the road.

I met with both of them individually to learn what the situation was and what the sore points were. I looked at the profit and loss statement so I could understand where they were financially and what the son was doing to earn his keep, as it were.

Once I was informed, I met with both of them in the same room and suggested the father reward his son's leadership by giving his son a small percentage of stock at the end of each fiscal year. As for the father's desire to help others, I suggested that the company start buying back the father's stock, which would provide more than sufficient funds for the father to become involved in other interests—and give the money away to charitable organizations. This move would also aid in the transition of ownership to the son.

Sometimes an entrepreneurial business can't make it—and coughs and sputters toward in inglorious end, which is another way of saying that your company wasn't able to generate sufficient cash flow to sustain the business. When you've reached this point and realize that the doors will have to close and close soon, you want to wind down the business with as little damage as possible, preserving assets if you can.

Sometimes there's so little business that the best option is to shut down the operation, sell off what you can, take a loss, and move on with your life, hopefully having learned a lot in the process. That happened to me in the automobile lending business to sub-prime borrowers that I described in Chapter 2. We sold at a low price to a bargain-hunting investor who specialized in turnarounds—and walked away from our financial wounds.

Or sometimes an unfortunate catastrophe hits unexpectedly, and you just have to buckle down and begin all over again. Erie Sauder, the founder of the Sauder Woodworking Company in

Archbold, Ohio, lost his entire manufacturing facility to a devastating fire in 1945 just as his business was beginning to bloom. Sauder's uncle also died in the blaze.

But Sauder never gave up. Against the odds, he found friends and bankers willing to take a risk with him. Sauder rebuilt his manufacturing facilities to become an outstanding corporation and the largest U.S. manufacturer of RTA or "ready to assemble" furniture today, employing over 2,500 employees. He also gave back to the Archbold community in many good ways, such as preserving the history and heritage of northwest Ohio in his formation of Sauder Village, now managed by his granddaughter.

Going Bust

I mentioned at the beginning of this book that start-up businesses have close to a 50 percent chance of not making it after five years in business, which is a swing in the right direction from 2011 when 57 percent of business closed their doors. Some of these businesses simply close their doors; others are absorbed into a larger company; and some have to file bankruptcy.

There are a zillion reasons why companies go BK—bankrupt. Sometimes markets shift so rapidly, especially in the Information Age, that the firm cannot adjust quickly enough to survive the turbulent market conditions. Most of the time, however, failures could have been prevented by paying more attention to critical factors in the business operation.

There are generally three types of bankruptcy:

• Chapter 7, which means the company throws in the towel and goes completely out of business. When the business is liquidated, creditors receive what's left, which is often pennies on the dollar.

- Chapter 11, which means the company needs to take a breather and work out a reorganization plan to get back on its feet.
- Chapter 13, which means provisions are made by the court to repay creditors in installments.

No entrepreneur likes to contemplate bankruptcy while doing business, but there are occasions when everyone recognizes that some companies didn't make it and ran out of money to keep going or pay off creditors.

Sometimes bankruptcy is the only option under certain unsustainable situations. If that is your only option, work with bankruptcy attorneys since there are legal requirements that must be followed. If your business has to shut down, don't beat yourself up. The important thing is to move on and learn from the experience, but remind yourself that trying and failing is better than never having tried at all.

Just because your business fails doesn't mean you're a failure or that you can't try again. In fact, I hope that I have readers of *Launching the Entrepreneurial Ship* who *have* gone BK because I want to tell you that it's not over—you can still make a comeback, you can still succeed.

I am reminded of the comeback story of Milton Hershey, who grew up in Lancaster's Mennonite community in the middle of the 19th century. When he was fourteen years old, he worked as an apprentice for a German-English newspaper, but he got fired when he dropped a tray of type. Then young Milton tried his hand at becoming a confectioner—someone who made candies. He apprenticed with a Lancaster confectioner named Joseph H. Royer and learned the candy-making trade.

Milton struck out on his own in 1876, when he was nineteen years old, and moved to Philadelphia. He sold homemade taffy and caramels from a pushcart and worked himself to exhaustion from making candy at night and selling confections by day. After six years, he threw in the towel and struck out for Denver, where he opened up a candy store. That failed, as did a new candy shop in Chicago. There were other confectionary stores, like ones in New York City and New Orleans, but those went belly-up as well.

And then Milton figured out a way to make milk chocolate, which was a closely guarded secret by Swiss chocolatiers. After perfecting his recipe, he was ready to make inexpensive "Hershey bars," which became a huge hit. He bought dairy land in Derry Church, about thirty miles from our home in Lancaster, and built a massive factory and a company town. Perhaps you've heard of Hershey, Pennsylvania.

Hershey amassed a fortune and was booked for passage on the R.M.S. *Titanic* but had to take an earlier crossing a few days before the *Titanic* began its ill-fated voyage. He and his wife, Kitty, had no children, so he spent the last years of his life (Hershey died in 1945 at the age of eighty-eight) involved in philanthropy. His foundation has funded hundreds of civic efforts, schools, orphanages, and scholarships over the decades with an endowment of $12 billion. Yes, billion.

The lesson to be learned here: If your entrepreneurial idea is a winner, keep a level head and keep moving forward. Sure, you might fail or have severe setbacks. But if you can somehow pick yourself up off the ground, learn from your experiences, and try, try again, the rewards could be awesome. And if your ship does come in, use your good fortune to do good to others.

FIFTEEN

When Your Ship Comes In

"You have to make sure your dream is inextricably linked to who you are."

—Ama Yawson, co-founder of Joojos,
an artisanal children's shoe company

"Ships are the nearest things to dreams that hands have ever made."

—Robert N. Rose, president and CEO of Rose Consulting

Have you been thinking about what kind of entrepreneur you want to become?

The reason I ask that question is because I've met plenty of entrepreneurs over the years who are so focused on starting their business and making it go that they lose sight of their purpose and their values.

This is why I keep harping on the value of developing and writing a Values Statement, which is a reminder of what type of company you want to lead. I'm sure you want to do your part to make this a better world—everyone would agree to that. The question becomes: *What can I do to make sure we're a socially conscious company when we're paddling like crazy to stay afloat?*

My answer: by being intentional about giving back, and by giving back when you can.

In fact, I'm hoping that throughout your entrepreneurial endeavor you will emphasize and practice corporate responsibility. That's a very important thing to include in your Values Statement and Mission Statement since putting that desire—in writing—defines your culture and says a lot about how you will run your business, what products and services you will provide, how you will provide them, and what you'll do with the money that comes in—if you're successful.

I'm fortunate to have been part of corporations and firms that generously gave back to the community, especially to the neighborhoods and schools where most of their employees lived. If you want motivated "team members," then let them work in an environment where they feel like they are working for something bigger than themselves.

I remember one company in which I consulted with the owner. I'll call him Dave. One day, I was asking him what his long-term goals were for his company. He looked at me and said without hesitation, "My purpose in business isn't to make a ton of money. I want to provide good jobs, and I want to be a good corporate citizen. I want to give back to the community."

"That's great to hear," I said. "I can help you write a good plan on how to do that."

I listened and took notes. Right from the beginning, Dave said he wanted his company to give 10 percent of their net income to charitable organizations. He said he was acting under the biblical mandate (in Malachi, the last book in the Old Testament) to give back to God 10 percent of what we make through our "tithes and offerings."

He had a question for me. "Can I afford to give 10 percent of my profits and still be a good businessman?" he asked.

I thought for a moment because I could see that this was a fork-in-the-road moment for Dave. "Yes, but you're going to trade a bit of company growth for making that happen," I said. "On the other hand, your employees will love what you're doing and will be motivated that much more. I could see them helping you become 10 percent more profitable a year from now."

Dave clapped his hands. "That's great," he said. "Let's do it."

The entrepreneur wasn't done yet. His next move was brilliant: he sent out an email to all his employees and said that at the end of the fiscal year, he wanted them to determine what worthy organizations would receive the money.

Dave only had a handful of employees at the time, so it was easy to gather everyone together to talk things through after the first year of operation. His new company showed a handsome $100,000 profit.

Dave looked around the conference room at his mostly male team. "Guys, we have $10,000 to contribute," he said. "What are your ideas?"

One of his employees raised his hand. "I'm involved with a bicycle repair shop for homeless men, and they could use new bike stands and tools," he said.

Bingo.

"Let's give them $2,500," Dave said.

Another raised his hand. "Our church is sending a dozen teens on a mission trip to Costa Rica this summer. They're raising money through bake sales and car washes."

Bingo.

"Let's give them $1,500," Dave said.

And so it went. Many worthwhile ministries and non-profit organizations were helped.

In coming years, as his company took off, Dave learned that you can't outgive God—so he gave more. He was like a friend who told me that he and his wife started giving 10 percent of their income when they got married, but agreed that if things went well, then they would increase that percentage.

Well, business was very good, so they upped their giving to 20 percent . . . to 30 percent . . . all the way to 90 percent of their income. This is known as a "reverse tithe"—meaning they were living off 10 percent of their income and giving away the rest.

Living this way was in a way a sacrifice for them. My friend could have bought a huge yacht and plied the Caribbean half the year, but he knew that material things don't last. "I want to invest in God's work here on this earth. That's something that has eternal ramifications," he said.

I am on board with what he said, and I try to practice what he preached. In my case, I can afford to drive a new Mercedes off the lot, but Doris and I aren't impressed with shiny expensive cars. I drive a Camry hybrid and feel good about that. Doris drives a ten-year-old Camry. We live in a modest house in Lancaster. Sure, we have a three-fourths of an acre, filled with beautiful flowers because of Doris' green thumb, but you won't find our home featured on the pages of *Architectural Digest*. That's because we choose to invest in Kingdom work. Having said that, I will confess to a weakness for traveling and taking expensive trips with the extended family accompanying us. In my stage of life, there's nothing better than picking up the tab for a Canadian trip to Jasper and the Columbia Icefield with our adult children and their families, or taking grandchildren on an African safari.

When we were raising our kids—this would be before the rise of SuperNet—we lived in a modest neighborhood, even though we could afford more, because we wanted our children to grow up "normal." One time, when Debbie was in elementary school, I used to get a lot of FedEx and UPS deliveries—usually contracts from investment bankers that needed to be signed. Because of all the deliveries, the kids in the neighborhood would tease my daughter about the "money trucks" that came to our house when she was in elementary school. That bothered her. I mean, it really upset her.

"The kids are teasing me because we're rich," she said one night at the dinner table.

Doris and I smiled at each other. "Honey," I said, "those aren't money trucks." And then my wife and I did our best to explain that the trucks that beat a path to our front door were delivery trucks, not money trucks, and they were delivering documents and packages, not bundles of cash.

What pleases me most is how money has been handled by my oldest son, Rod. He became a millionaire at age thirty-three, but you'd never know it by the way he chooses to live. Sure, he has a nice home, but he drives a Ford Explorer and chooses to spend his money on Christian schooling for his kids and stay away from a conspicuous lifestyle.

I'm very, very proud of him, as well as my son Jeff and daughter Deb, who live similarly.

Giving Back to the Community

One of the beauties of family businesses—even those that are national in scope—is that they often invest in their local community. They do so because they live there, their children go to local schools, and they socialize and worship with friends in their neighborhood. They support the arts, worthwhile charities, and upstanding causes doing good work in their neighborhood. My observation has been large corporations, multi-state firms, and public companies generally give back less to their communities than family-owned businesses.

Besides the psychic benefit of seeing so much good done at the local level, donating to local community groups and nonprofits is also a business write-off, if I can be so crass. To me, the tax deduction—up to one-third off your gross income—is an incentive that the U.S. and state governments have written into the tax code, so don't be shy about using that law to your advantage.

Some firms make social responsibility a fun part of their corporate culture, which I strongly endorse. A great example is Timberland, a manufacturer of outdoor men's and woman's clothing and footwear, originally operating in New Hampshire and Maine. Back in 1992, Timberland began a "Path to Service Program" where the entire company focused on a paid day off in which employees divided up into teams and performed a day of service for their communities.

In 1997, Timberland expanded the scope of their service day, calling their program "Serv-a-palooza" after the "Lollapalooza" music festivals. Today, this program has exploded to two focused days of service, one in the spring and one in the fall, in which 1,500 employees complete roughly seventy service projects in more than ten countries. An example would be a transformational urban greening project in New York City or cleaning parks in China or the United Kingdom. In the last twenty-five years, more than 1,000,000 trees have been planted, schools have been renovated, and care packages have been delivered to seniors.

Timberland's "Earthkeepers" have developed a culture of serving needs within their communities and turned the service day into a fun program. And the outdoor lifestyle brand is striving to make it even better. They have a team of thirty green-shirted employees from nineteen countries called "Global Stewards" who volunteer above and beyond their regular job responsibilities to serve others in their communities. Timberland also pays employees up to forty hours annually to volunteer in ways that speak to their own passion.

While you likely won't be able to sponsor a program as elaborate or sophisticated as Timberland, give your employees the opportunity to share their socially responsible ideas with your management team. This could become a defining part of your company culture, as it has for Timberland, which has reaped wonderful publicity for this initiative. I also want to add that many Millennials respond favorably to this type of company culture.

Another approach to consider in managing your charitable giving, especially if you are in a cyclical industry, is to form a foundation where you can contribute money in the good years and pull back in the lean years. By building up the balances when business is good, you can be more consistent in giving to causes you want to support over the long haul. This enables the receiving parties to receive steady donations from your endeavors, as opposed to feast-and-famine support. And here's another idea: if you're husbanding cash and can't afford to make a donation, you can offer your product or service at cost as a way of giving back.

Setting up a charitable foundation, no matter how much or how little you use it, is a good business practice. Having a foundation in place gives you the opportunity to donate stock with a low basis from a sale right into the foundation. This is a good way to minimize taxes and build a longer-term charitable vehicle and can even be an important element in estate planning.

In our case, after EarthLink bought us out, our family established the Lefever Family Foundation. We were advised that if and when we sold our EarthLink stock, that money would be subject to a sizable capital gains tax. But by giving that stock to the Lefever Foundation and *then* selling it, that money was not subject to any taxes, which meant we could distribute donations to charitable organizations from our foundation. Doris and I were gratified to sponsor several college scholarships for students from

Eastern Europe to LCC International University in Lithuania. Another recipient was the Mennonite Economic Development Associates (MEDA), which invests in the lives of families living in poverty around the world. (I describe how we became involved with LCC International and MEDA in my next chapter.) It really is better to give than to receive.

One of the unexpected side benefits to having a family foundation was being able to name our three children and their spouses (as they got married) as directors in our family foundation, teaching them the joy of giving. It also provided a financial source that would enable our children and their spouses to support causes they believed in. They could utilize $1,000 annually to fund a ministry or nonprofit group they wanted to support. I remember Debbie and her husband, Ross, using the money to help start a bicycle repair business for homeless men, which was tremendous.

When Debbie was a teen, she went through a period where she ran with some friends who generally viewed business as bad, that businessmen were often greedy, and capitalism was a questionable system. You could say that she became anti-money.

She'd help her friends do a bake sale for a local farmer's market project start-up and net $75 or maybe a couple of hundred dollars at the most. But at the tip of her fingers was the ability to give $1,000 to help get the project off the ground.

Writing that check really helped her appreciate that money can be used for the good of society.

A Cautionary Tale

Let's say your entrepreneurial idea takes off. Let's say you're a savvy businessperson who makes a lot of money. Let's say that you become rich from your entrepreneurial idea.

I now share a story, both good and sad, about wealth:

When we consolidated thirty-three Internet companies in the late '90s, many of the owners were relatively young individuals. They had the good fortune of being in college in 1993, 1994, or 1995 as the Internet was making waves.

Upon graduation, they returned to their small or mid-sized hometowns, where they found that there was no Internet service yet. So, out of a sense of frustration or feeling entrepreneurial like Rod, Carlton, and myself, they saw an opportunity to launch their own ISP. They bought a few routers, connected with their local phone company, and they were in business.

Their ISPs grew rapidly, and in many cases, the young entrepreneurs hired their buddies as their first employees, who were naturally given more responsibilities as the company gained customers. Everyone worked for peanuts, including the owners, because rapid growth required capital, but hanging on to a launching rocket ship was fun.

During those heady days, the value of these ISPs rose like a moonshot. In quite a few cases, these young owners were sitting on a company worth anywhere from $4 million to $10 million dollars. That was on paper. In reality, they were cash poor.

As these young owners approached their late twenties, they began to get married, start families, and buy their first homes. For them, the time was ripe to cash out. Our offer of an attractive exit, with an on-going opportunity for them to continue to run their Internet business as part of our new team, was appealing to nearly everyone.

In 2001, when EarthLink bought OneMain.com, around seventy-one persons became overnight millionaires, as I mentioned in Chapter 1. A number of these relatively young persons did some incredibly wonderful things with these newfound riches. Some started some new businesses, others purchased homes for their parents or paid their siblings' student loans. One person almost single-handedly donated enough money for their small town high school to build a new gym.

Then there were those who squandered their fortune. One group went wild by purchasing the on-the-floor season tickets for the Sacramento Kings, an NBA franchise, and partied like it was, well, 1999. Alcohol and drugs ruined them.

The saddest tale, though, was about a young man I'll call Scott, whom I loved. He was a fiery entrepreneur with incredible potential. After the EarthLink sale made him a wealthy young man, he went out and bought a new Mercedes to celebrate—as well as hot cars for his friends. They went out drinking one Saturday night, got into some street racing, and the next thing Scott knew, he lost control of his car at high speed, crashed, and died. What a loss! I grieve every time I think of this outcome.

Don't squander your money on an extravagant lifestyle that you can afford today but may not afford tomorrow or next year. Have a rainy-day fund on the side. Money should be looked at as a means to do good things for your family and for others, which will bring you more satisfaction than playing golf every day.

The lesson to be learned here: When your ship finally comes in, how will you handle the wealth from your cargo? Hopefully your Values Statement, your practice of Corporate Social Responsibility, your sense of stewardship, and your moral compass will be your guiding principles.

SIXTEEN

Putting It All Together

"The best things in life are the people we love, the places we've been, the dreams we've fulfilled, and the memories we've made along the way."

—Allon Lefever, author of this book

Ah, the entrepreneurial life.

It's the life I've lived, and it's the life I've loved.

I described my ancestors' story in Chapter 7 about how my great-great-whatever- grandfather Isaac Lefever took an enormous risk by coming to the New World in 1706 on a rickety sailing ship that crossed the Atlantic Ocean—a dangerous endeavor. He eventually settled in Lancaster County, Pennsylvania, and built a life for himself and his family with practically his bare hands and a few farm tools.

His entrepreneurial spirit was passed along to succeeding generations, which I'm part of. As we sail into port at the end of our journey about entrepreneurship, I want to talk about the Lefevers who directly impacted who I became and who I am today—and the lessons we can learn from them.

My grandfather, Harry Lefever, was an excellent role model while I grew up. Following the end of World War II, he successfully turned his tomato-growing operation into a commercial flower business. But when his equally entrepreneurial-minded son—my father, Elvin, wanted to expand operations and start wholesaling carnation flowers in Philadelphia, my grandfather worked with my father to make that happen. In fact, Dad oversaw the construction of several greenhouses that totaled 22,000 square feet, or half an acre, and he successfully staked out territory in the competitive commercial flower market in the City of Brotherly Love.

Growing up, I was expected to help out with the family flower business. Here I'm in one of our six greenhouses with my younger brothers, Ray and David, standing next to carnations grown for the wholesale market in Philadelphia.

Meanwhile, my grandfather continued to grow vegetables like tomatoes and corn on the side and deliver his produce to a central market in Lancaster. If that wasn't enough, he also owned and managed several apartment complexes *and* was a Mennonite pastor on Sunday mornings, for which he received no salary. I'm telling you, he was a remarkable man.

I'll never forget accompanying Grandpa when he needed help tidying up the grounds of apartments he owned. I saw how my grandfather interacted with kindness and respect toward the tenants. On the ride home, while I licked on an ice cream he bought me for helping out, I heard him tell me that everyone needed to be treated with dignity.

Our family attended Grandpa's Mennonite church, of course, since he was the pastor. Before I came along, Dad was a conscientious objector in World War II because of his Mennonite faith. One of the trademark characteristics of Mennonites is their commitment to pacifism because of their fundamental belief that war is never the answer to solving the world's problems. This was not a popular position in the early 1940s, especially after the Pearl Harbor attack led us to declare war on Japan and its Axis partner, Nazi Germany.

Dad did his part for the war effort by working at Greystone Park Psychiatric Hospital in Morris Plains, New Jersey. He and a lot of other young Mennonite men—all conscientious objectors— wound up as orderlies in hospitals or counselors in children's homes because the draft boards that assigned them knew it wouldn't be easy duty.

When Dad and the other Mennonite COs saw how horribly the staff treated mental patients, they were dispirited. Mentally disturbed patients were verbally and physically abused, and many received electroshock therapy that prompted convulsions until they were knocked unconscious. Others were lobotomized, a surgical procedure in which nerve tracts in the frontal lobe of the brain were severed to "calm" the patient.

When the war was over and the Mennonite conscientious objectors returned to civilian life, many believed there had to be a better way to provide professional care for the mentally ill other than what they saw in those disturbing mental health institutions. They started talking among themselves about what they could do for the mentally ill. In the late 1940s, a dozen Mennonite colleagues, including my father, approached the Lancaster Conference of Bishops that oversee the area churches and said: "We would like to open a facility that treats the mentally ill better."

Talk about being entrepreneurial. Who would have the thought—or have the audacity, if I can use that word—to build and operate a mental hospital for the less fortunate? But my father and his Mennonite friends did, and they were serious about starting this worthwhile ministry.

After receiving an okay from the Conference of Bishops, a campaign raised enough money to construct Philhaven, a mental hospital in Lebanon County forty miles to the north of Lancaster. When it came time to hire an administrator, the Conference leaders looked around and said to my father: *We think you are the one to run Philhaven.*

I'm at the left, holding a bunch of cut carnations next to my uncle Paul, my mother Mary, and my father Elvin.

"No, no, no," my father said. "I'm not trained for this. Besides, I have my greenhouse operation and I'd have to move the family to Lebanon County."

Despite those formidable hurdles, the Mennonite leaders eventually talked my father into taking the hospital administrator position with the promise that they would continue the search for a suitable candidate to take my father's place sometime down the road.

We moved to Lebanon County, and my dad's brother, Uncle Paul, took over the greenhouse operation back in Lancaster. Philhaven's doors opened on May 7, 1952, a time I remember well because I was finishing up kindergarten. Philhaven started as a twenty-six-bed facility with outpatient and community education services.

We spent two years in Lebanon County until the Lancaster Conference of Bishops located a suitable administrator to take Dad's place. What he did serving the mentally ill was a huge illustration of following a call and giving back to the least of these. Our time in Lebanon County would impact me in many ways.

A Sweetheart Deal

Like many children of farmers or growers, I was expected to help out. I guess I never knew a time when I didn't have a set of chores, but don't get the wrong idea—my parents weren't slave drivers. Mom and Dad allowed me plenty of time to hang out with my friends and have a wonderful childhood.

As a teenager, I attended Lancaster Mennonite High School, a private school affiliated with the Mennonite Church. For the Lancaster area, we were a fairly large high school with about 150 students in each class. In my junior year, I noticed a cute brunette named Doris Blank. We liked each other immediately but our parents told us we were too young to date. Though we could still see each other, we weren't allowed to hold hands! Instead, we played ping-pong in the school Rec Hall.

We were allowed to date during our senior year. By then, we were hopelessly in love, as many high school sweethearts are. My parents knew a married couple who were several years older than us, Christian and Laverne Peifer, and they encouraged us to hang out with them. They became mentors because our parents allowed us to meet at their place, almost as chaperones. The Peifers had a mural of a mountain in their kitchen, and we would always talk about what was on the other side of the mountain. Although none of us knew what was in our future, it was fun for Doris and me to dream about being together, starting a family, and doing life together.

One evening, Christian and I were discussing how much we liked playing softball. But there wasn't any sort of organized league in Lancaster, and impromptu after-church softball games were always played on makeshift fields that didn't have infields or outfield fences.

Hey, why don't we build a real softball field and start our own church softball league?

I can't remember who spoke up first, but we both liked the idea.

Christian and I approached a local elementary school and asked if we could use some of their land to build a softball field. We were about to be politely turned down when we mentioned that our group had raised enough money to put up an outfield fence and lights for night play. We also said we had a friend with a bulldozer who'd scrape out an infield for us.

The following spring, we were playing softball. We had enough people sign up to field ten teams, which gave us a kitty to maintain the field. I had a ball running the church softball league, which led me to start a bowling league that is still going strong today. (My brother, Raymond, still bowls in the same league more than fifty years later.)

When I graduated from Lancaster Mennonite High with the Class of '64, I was handed more than a diploma: I also received a notice from the Selective Service System notifying me that I would be drafted into the U.S. Army.

Talk about a huge shock. Although the Korean War had ended in 1953, the Selective Service System still conducted a "peacetime" draft during the Cold War, inducting 120,000 men each year. But the Vietnam War was heating up in Southeast Asia, and my number got called.

Being a Mennonite pacifist allowed me to claim conscientious objector status, but my draft board ordered me to work in a home for emotionally disturbed children in Albany, New York, as part of my alternative service. Doris got a summer job working for DuPont in Wilmington, Delaware, while I worked as a counselor at Albany Home for Children, a residential facility.

Since the kids attended an on-property school during the day, I had breaks in my day, which gave me time to enroll in several psychology and economics classes at nearby Russell Sage University. Then, in the late afternoon and early evenings, I would help the emotionally challenged children with their schoolwork, get them bathed and fed, and see them off to bed, for which I was paid a modest salary. I then donated the salary to the Eastern Mennonite Board of Missions to support other community assistance projects.

I can't tell you how homesick I was to see Doris or even talk to her. Don't forget that in the mid-1960s, long distance phone calls were expensive. I could only afford a five-minute call once a week, so we made every minute count. At the end of the summer, I asked Doris to marry me, and she accepted. We planned for a March wedding.

We married when we were both nineteen. It was probably a Mennonite thing. A lot of our church friends got married out of high school because they didn't go to college in those days. They planned to work on the family farm, or go into construction, waitress in a restaurant, or become a store clerk. As for me, my game plan was to go into the family business with my father after high school and not go to college. I had spoken with Dad about doubling the number of greenhouses and pursuing a much bigger share of the carnation market in Pennsylvania, but then I received my draft notice.

After our two-day honeymoon in New York, Doris joined me for my second year in Albany, where we got an apartment and settled into married life. I continued my counseling duties with the emotionally disturbed children and took more classes at Russell Sage University. Suddenly, we were hit by a major surprise: Doris was pregnant. Rod was born in 1966 in Albany, and the responsibilities of being a father weighed heavily on my shoulders.

When my two-year alternative service commitment was up, we moved back to our hometown. Dad and I resurrected the idea of building another greenhouse, but since my departure to New York, the wholesale flower business had slipped. That development, coupled with my exposure to a broader world as well as business classes at Russell Sage University, steered me in the direction of going to college and earning a degree.

I enrolled at Millersville University, a liberal arts state university just outside of Lancaster. Married, with a child, and working part time with my father to support our young family, I didn't have time for the hippie antiwar protests that swept across college campuses in the late Sixties. I did grow my hair out a bit and owned a pair of purple bellbottoms, however.

I kept my nose to the grindstone as I pursued an undergraduate degree in social studies with an emphasis in economics. Though it took me several extra semesters to complete the required course work at Millersville, I graduated magna cum laude in 1971. I also received a top economics award for surveying a number of banks in Lancaster County as part of a research project.

Now I had the education bug. I wanted to go on to graduate school and earn a doctorate because I wanted to teach economics at the college level some day or become a corporate economist. With that goal in mind, as well as Doris' backing, I was accepted into Penn State's Ph.D. program in economics, thanks to the recommendation I received from Dr. M.K. Hamid, the dean of the Social Sciences department at Millersville University.

When I started my doctorate program, Penn State's economics department was ranked No. 38 in the country, which I learned would likely not be good enough to become a college professor at a top school. As for becoming a corporate economist, those jobs were disappearing because corporations weren't hiring economists in-house any longer.

One snowy evening, Doris and I drove to Roundtop Mountain to have dinner and discuss what we should do. While we watched the night skiers come down the slopes from our restaurant table, a thick blanket of snowflakes fell outside, creating a beautiful winter scene.

"I don't think it makes sense for me to go for a Ph.D.," I said. "Four more years of schooling, tuition costs, plus we want to have more children . . . ." My voice trailed off.

"You know I'll support you in whatever you decide," Doris said. She'd always been my biggest booster and had a heart of gold.

"That's wonderful to hear, but I think I need to drop out of the doctorate program."

"Really?"

"Yes, for the reasons I just laid out. But I could go for a master's degree in economics from Penn State instead. That would only take another year and look great on my résumé. What do you think of that?"

Doris reacted positively. "That sounds great," she said.

I reached for Doris's hand, and we were in agreement. We made the mutual decision for me to pursue a master's degree.

It wasn't long after that when Doris got pregnant with our second son Jeff, so we had a lot going on. After I graduated with my master's in 1973, I spoke with Dad about my future in the commercial flower business, which was continuing to slide in the wrong direction. Refrigerated aircraft were delivering tons of flowers from South America in advance of Valentine's Day, Mother's Day, and the early summer wedding season, which really cut into our profits. Labor costs were shooting up as well.

My wife, Doris, has a great sense of humor. Of course, we hope this doesn't happen, but we are committed to each other if it does!

Then in the fall of 1973, following the Arab-Israeli War, the Organization of Petroleum Exporting Countries (OPEC) slapped an oil embargo on the United States in response to our support of Israel during the Yom Kippur War. The price of oil quadrupled from $3 a barrel to $12 a barrel—a long way from what we pay today but still sending shock waves through the economy. My father used to buy heating oil for 10 cents a gallon to keep the greenhouses warm. Suddenly, the price shot up to fifty, eighty, ninety cents a gallon.

Dad and I had been talking about building an eighty-by-two-hundred-foot greenhouse—a twin to the largest greenhouse we had—but he had stopped showing me the numbers on how the business was doing. If there was anything I learned over seven years of higher education, it was the balance sheet revealed everything. I was worried about approaching my father, but I finally mustered the courage to tell him that I didn't think it was a good idea to add another greenhouse to the property.

"You know, I've been thinking the same thing," he said to my relief. "I think you're right. We shouldn't build the addition."

That was a smart decision because the market for wholesale flowers was continuing its downward trend. The cost of heating the greenhouses in winter was getting prohibitive, and we couldn't compete against bigger domestic greenhouse operations and foreign growers who had economies of scale working in their favor.

Dad gave me his blessing to go out on my own and see what the world had to offer. I was probably the first Lefever not to follow his father's footsteps in a long time, but Dad wisely recognized that at the age of twenty-seven, I was ready to pave my own path. Victor F. Weaver, Inc. hired me quickly as a corporate training manager, and from that humble start, I was steadily promoted until I assumed overall responsibility for the Operations division of the company in just seven years. At the age of thirty-four, I had reached the executive suite in the corporate world.

In 1986, after Weaver was sold to Holly Farms, I resigned and joined High Industries, Inc., which gave me another boost up the corporate ladder. As I rose to senior vice president at High Industries, I was given the task to find or start new companies that would exhibit high growth rates and be less capital intensive than some of High Industries' other companies. The new companies I started helped revenue grow from $200 million to $400 million, and profits improved.

And then there was the story of SuperNet. By now, you're familiar with how SuperNet was a start-up ISP in 1993 and how eight years later we were part of the mega-successful sale of OneMain.com to EarthLink in 2001 for $308 million. That's when you could say my ship came in.

I stayed on with EarthLink, but after six months of nonstop travel searching for more ISPs to purchase on EarthLink's behalf, I decided that I didn't want to be away from my family that much. Working for a *really* big corporation was an eye-opener as well. It was time to move on. To what, I didn't know.

I had a few business ideas, but none were materializing. I thought back to the days when I had contemplated teaching Economics in the college classroom, but I had let that dream go when I dropped out of the Ph.D. program at Penn State.

Right around this time, a friend recommended that I read *Halftime: Changing Your Game Plan from Success to Significance* by Bob Buford. The premise of his book was that guys approaching the "halftime" of life—middle age—should take an "intermission" to contemplate a transition from seeking success to making a quest for significance in the second half of life.

The message of *Halftime* hit me like a ton of bricks. I pondered several questions posed by Buford, including these:

1. What are you really good at?
2. Where do you want to go from today to the end of your life?
3. What is most important to you?
4. What do you want to be remembered for?
5. If you could do anything you wanted for the rest of your life, what would that be?

Buford's unique book was perfect timing for me. For twenty years, I had the good fortune of working as a senior manager in two well-run and profitable businesses owned by Christian families dedicated to good values and ethical behavior in their business practices. Then I had the good fortune to support my son and join him in our "family business"—if I can stretch the definition for a moment.

We had been lucky, or fortunate, to launch SuperNet in the midst of a disrupting technological breakthrough. I also had the opportunity to take six companies public on Wall Street in the crazy '90s and been privileged to serve on over sixty boards of directors, ranging from privately held companies to non-profits and foundations.

On the personal side, Doris and I had a wonderful marriage, our three children were mature adults marrying and forming their own families, and we had welcomed our first grandchild to this world. We could count on dozens and dozens of close friends throughout the U.S. and in Canada and Europe.

So what was I going to do in the second half of my life? I understood I had a unique God-given opportunity to use my experience, management skills, and background in the business world in a different way.

One thing that kept me busy was serving on boards of directors, and one of those boards was with Goshen College, a small Christian institute of higher learning in Goshen, Indiana. I first became involved with the school when my son, Rod, earned his undergraduate degree at Goshen back in the mid-1980s.

Following the board meetings on the Goshen campus, I was sometimes asked to lecture to the business students about topics like how to start up a business from scratch, what should go into a business plan, what investors are looking for, and what it means to take a company public. On these occasions, I got to know some of the business faculty members.

Not long after EarthLink purchased OneMain.com, I received a call from Goshen's president, Shirley Showalter.

"I saw in *USA Today* that your company sold to EarthLink," she began. "Congratulations. That was quite a feat."

"Thank you, Shirley. We're all still on cloud nine. What happened is really unbelievable, but it took a lot of work to get there. We're thankful for what the Lord has done."

"So what's next?" she asked.

"Well, EarthLink wanted me to assist them in acquiring more ISPs. I wasn't sure if this was something I wanted to do because of all the travel, but they wanted me to give it a try for six months and see how it goes. That's where we are right now."

"So you don't know if you'll be staying with EarthLink long term?"

I sighed. "I don't think I'm cut out for EarthLink, but like I said, they asked me to stay with the company during the transition time, and I said I would."

"Would you consider making a major career change? Because if you are, we have an opening for teaching in our business department and directing the college's outreach to the local business community. We're calling it the Family Business Institute, and we think you'd be the perfect person to lead this effort."

I was flattered and told Shirley so. I thought about Bob Buford's book *Halftime* and wondered if the book's message was for me.

"You've given me something to think about," I said. "I'm going to have to talk to Doris, and I still have my situation at EarthLink." I mentioned that I was thinking about accepting EarthLink's severance package.

"You take your time," Shirley said. "We can wait a bit longer. We'd love to have you."

As I described earlier, I decided to accept EarthLink's severance package, but as Doris and I talked about accepting Goshen's offer, I wasn't sure that a move from eastern Pennsylvania and from our six-month-old grandson (who lived only a mile away from us, I might add) to Goshen six hundred miles away to step into the academic world was really my calling.

I told Shirley that in a follow-up phone call, noting that I liked the idea of impacting the lives of young persons contemplating careers in business, but I wasn't quite sure of either the geographic move or the entrance into the academic world. I asked her if I could give her a final decision after Doris and I attended the annual convention for the Mennonite Economic Development Associates (MEDA), an international economic development organization whose mission is to create business solutions to poverty. The Goshen College president said yes.

Doris and I had financially supported MEDA for years and participated in foreign trips. We'd flown to far-flung places like Ethiopia or Nicaragua and met with budding entrepreneurs who received microloans from MEDA to launch a business like processing grains or opening a zip line on the edge of a jungle for a growing tourist industry.

The annual MEDA conferences were held in major U.S. cities and offered thought-provoking speakers and excellent workshops. I always found the MEDA conventions to be a stimulating time because I got to rub shoulders with other businesspeople who were serious about integrating their faith into their business practices.

At any rate, at the 2001 MEDA convention, I prayed that God would give me some sort of a sign of what to do. I decided that if someone I knew came up to me with a business proposition, then I'd take that as an indication from the Lord that I should go to work for a new company and stay in the business world. On the other hand, if someone I knew came up to me and told me what a great teacher I'd make, then I would take that as a heavenly indicator to pack up and move to Goshen.

What I was doing was praying for some form of fleece—just as Gideon did in the Old Testament—as a sign from God spelling out exactly what I should do.

The convention was a good one, as it is every year, but disappointedly there was no fleece. As we were flying back to Pennsylvania that Sunday evening, I felt disappointed that God had not given me any sign of what to do.

When we got home, there were a number of messages on our phone answering machine. One was from a friend named Jim inviting me to a fund-raising breakfast at a nearby restaurant the next morning. He said the new headmaster of Philadelphia Mennonite School, a start-up Christian high school in Philadelphia's inner city, would be speaking.

"I'm having a tough time getting people to come to the breakfast," Jim said. "I hope you can make it."

I looked at my BlackBerry. I didn't have any appointments for the next morning, which was unusual. But it was 10 p.m.—a little late to call Jim. Should I phone him anyway and see if he still needed bodies or just let it go? I decided to call, despite the late hour. Sure enough, he picked up and begged me to come if possible, so I committed.

We gathered the following morning in a small meeting room at Bird-in-Hand Family Restaurant in nearby Bird-in-Hand. Following breakfast, we listened to Barbara Moses, the Philadelphia Mennonite School headmaster, tell her story. She had been a schoolteacher and administrator in Philadelphia's public school system for twenty-eight years and needed just two more years for a significantly better retirement package when suddenly she was offered the headmaster position at Philadelphia Mennonite, a start-up Christian high school.

"Although it didn't make sense to walk away from a much better pension plan, I felt the Lord was calling me to this new school—"

—whoops, my phone rang. I had forgotten to turn off my Blackberry. Embarrassed at disrupting others, I shot a glance at my screen and saw the call was coming from the 574 area code—which would mean Goshen. I excused myself and stepped out of the room to accept the call.

On the line was the human resources director of Goshen College. He was checking in to see if I had made a decision about their offer since I had said I would get back to them after the MEDA conference. I guess they were in more of a hurry than I thought.

"I'm in a meeting and will have to call you back," I said, stalling for time.

When I reentered the room, I heard Barbara conclude her talk by saying she hadn't looked back on her decision to leave the public school system. "Why was that?" she said. "Because I felt like I was part of something greater—educating inner city teens from a Christian perspective."

Barbara ended her talk by quoting from the Book of Joshua: "Have I not commanded you? Be strong and courageous. Do not be afraid; do not be discouraged, for the Lord your God will be with you wherever you go" (Joshua 1:9, NIV).

Well, you could hear a pin drop when she finished—followed by a thumping . . . an inner calling—in my chest.

I sat in my chair dumbfounded. What were the odds of:

• actually having a breakfast slot open, a rarity for me

• almost not bothering to call Jim back on Sunday night

• forgetting to turn off the Blackberry when I sat down for breakfast

• hearing Joshua 1:9 read out loud—a verse that perfectly fit the situation I was going through

The thought came to mind that God had just given me a clear sign—the fleece I was looking for regarding whether to take the position at Goshen College. Maybe it wasn't a fleece I expected or asked for but it was still in bright neon lights nonetheless. In other words, He was giving me a sign on His terms.

I went home from breakfast and told Doris what happened. We had been discussing Goshen's offer and the implications of moving for a good month, but this time we looked into each other's eyes and both *knew* that God was leading us to Goshen College. Other doors opened almost miraculously.

That morning, I called back the Goshen's HR director and said I decided to accept Goshen's offer. In short order, we put our house on the market and packed up for Indiana, where I became the Director of the Goshen College Family Business Institute and began teaching classes on Entrepreneurship, Principles of Management, and Family Business Succession.

The move to Goshen was fun and adventuresome, and the transition from the world of business to the world of academics was as smooth as I could hope for. I'll admit that relocating to

Indiana was more difficult for my wife, who missed holding our new grandchild. We made sure we were frequent visitors to Lancaster to see the little guy, Ben Lefever, as well as our children and their spouses, a high priority for us. I also remained on several boards in the Lancaster area, and we kept an apartment in a complex we owned.

Although working at Goshen College was a good experience, I found the pace of decision-making to be quite slow compared to the Internet world as well as the business realm I knew so well. I chalked it up to the good Lord knowing I needed grace in that "fruit of the Spirit" called patience.

My greatest joy came from interacting with the students, particularly the young idealists in my classes who heard me say that business was a worthy calling because of its potential to provide jobs, bring dignity to people, and to do good in the world. I was surprised to discover that so many entered college with a negative view of business. This prevailing attitude, I surmised, came from Hollywood movies and TV shows showing businessmen as schmucks and villains, pursuing profits at the expense of others. Capitalism was rarely shown in a positive light.

Two years in, we were rolling along at Goshen College when I received a call from the HR person at Eastern Mennonite University in Harrisonburg, Virginia. EMU, a small Christian liberal arts school similar to Goshen College, was looking for a new director of their MBA program.

I was happy at Goshen, but this out-of-the-blue feeler from Eastern Mennonite seemed like an excellent fit for my skill set. After speaking with Doris, I decided to apply, hoping to be offered the job. One of the big draws was that joining the EMU faculty and moving to Harrisonburg would put us a three-and-a-half-hour drive south of Lancaster.

I was offered the job as EMU's Director of the MBA Program and was also asked to teach Entrepreneurship to those in the MBA Program as well as to the undergraduates. I also taught Management and Strategy classes in the undergraduate program.

Heading up an MBA program on a college campus opened up numerous opportunities to lecture at conferences and other settings. I also began some consulting on the side. Numerous board opportunities came my way, so I said yes to ones that enhanced my ability to network on behalf of MBA students at EMU.

I gave EMU five years and left their MBA program in great shape when I decided to retire at the age of sixty-two in 2008. I wasn't planning to sit in a rocking chair, however. I wanted to continue serving on various boards, do more consulting, and have time to be involved in several small businesses.

That said, I look back on my seven years in the academic world with great satisfaction. Experience in both worlds—business and academia—gave me a broad perspective. The rewards in education were not nearly as tangible as in business, but the opportunity to share my real-world experiences and the chance to impact young lives was stimulating as well as rewarding. I'm still in contact with many of my students, and it's a joy to see them making meaningful contributions to making this a better world. Eight of them have now started their own businesses.

Equally rewarding are the new activities that I have today. My goal is to give more than one-third of my board service time to charitable or non-profit boards of directors. This opportunity to serve has been one of the most rewarding and fulfilling aspects of my life, other than my family, of course.

I will share briefly a few of these undertakings:

• In my earlier years, I was the chairman of the Habitat for Humanity chapter in Lancaster and got to personally know Millard and Linda Fuller, the founders of Habitat for Humanity, whenever they would come and speak at our annual fund-raising event. I have great respect for the vision and dedication of Millard and Linda Fuller. When Millard left Habitat for Humanity, he founded a second organization focused on helping persons have a decent home. A friend of mine became the chairman of the board of this new organization called the Fuller Center for Housing. I was honored to be asked to serve on this board.

Unfortunately, Millard passed away in 2009 at the age of seventy-four, so helping his infant organization go forward was a challenging experience. I had the opportunity to travel to other countries to help with "blitz builds"—where a number of houses and dozens of volunteers build a lot of houses in a week. Witnessing the joy and appreciation of the families receiving these homes is something I can close my eyes and relive any time I want.

• I have had the incredible privilege to serve on the MEDA Board of Directors for nine years and chair the board for two of those years. This organization works with the poor to bring hope, training, and capital to families in over two dozen countries around the world.

MEDA, as I mentioned earlier, invests heavily in micro-lending. Again, I've had the pleasure of meeting with families and farmers who've been the beneficiaries of these loans. I've visited MEDA's projects in Nicaragua, Paraguay, Tanzania, Ukraine, Crimea, and Tajikistan. The appreciation expressed to our team for the micro-lending and employment opportunities has been heartwarming.

In the Central Asian country of Tajikistan, I loved meeting this farmer who could clear twelve hectares of farmland for fruits and vegetables with this tractor obtained from a microloan provided by the Mennonite Economic Development Associates, of which I'm a board member.

• One of my most rewarding involvements came unexpectedly. I was asked to travel to LCC International University in Klaipėda, Lithuania, to do some lectures on Entrepreneurship and how I integrate my faith into the way I do business. A business friend, Myrl Nofsinger, joined me on the trip, and we shared our stories at a Tuesday afternoon school assembly that was open to all students.

At the conclusion of our presentation, LCC's president shared that following dinner Myrl and I would be available to informally meet with students in a dorm conference room. He also said that students could sign up for twenty-minute sessions with us during the next week.

Myrl and I jokingly wondered if any students would show up. I'll never forget the scene that evening as we walked into the conference room packed with eager students. They drilled us for ninety minutes with questions about the way we do business and what we look for. The next day and all that week, we were booked solid with twenty-minute one-on-ones with the students.

Invariably, the first question we heard at each appointment was "How do you do business in the West?" Their keen interest in learning was incredible. That worthwhile experience led to an invitation to serve on LCC's board of directors, which was the most international board I've ever served on. We were a board made up of Americans, Canadians, Germans, Ukrainians, and Russians.

I love making new friends on ministry trips, including this pastor of the Peace Church in Tbilisi, the capital of the Eurasian country of Georgia.

The board reflected the diverse student population, which was 60 percent international. The students come from twenty-six countries, and over 60 percent are business majors. That said, it was heartening to see Ukrainian students sharing dorm rooms with Russian students. (For the last few years, relations between Russia and Ukraine have been on a war footing since Russia annexed Crimea in 2014.)

Not only was I inspired by these students and LCC's dedicated faculty, but when I served as the chairman of this board, I got involved with an effort to partner with a Christian academic endeavor in St. Petersburg, Russia. On the down side, we were working with a Christian university in Donetsk, in the eastern part of Ukraine, but that university closed down when separatists overran the campus, overtook the dormitories, and gave the students and faculty forty-eight hours to leave. So sad!

These involvements—as well as new relationships, new exposure to cultures, and opportunities to make a difference in future leaders in a part of the world that desperately needs ethical and competent leadership has meant a great deal to me. To follow the LCC graduates and see the impact they are making in Ukraine and in their home countries has been incredibly fulfilling. I was the one transformed, along with the students.

• Finally, I recently joined the board of the Museum of the Bible, located in Washington, D.C. just three blocks from the White House. Anyone who looks to the Bible for their inspiration, or anyone who wishes to engage with the Bible, is welcome to the table. I've enjoyed working side-by-side with the Jewish, Catholic, and Protestant faith communities, which has given me a new appreciation for the traditions and integrity of these faiths as we construct a 430,000-square foot high-tech Museum of the Bible.

A Final Thought

I understand that I'm entering the twilight of my career and my life.

I love where I am and value time with my family even more. My life is richer because of my wife, Doris, our three children and their spouses, and the ten grandchildren we're blessed with. We love every one of them. I value the opportunity to help others through my small consulting business and take great delight in serving on various boards.

Why take risks in life? One reason is to provide a better future for our children and our grandchildren, who joined us for a memorable family vacation at the Columbia Ice Fields in Canada.

As I look back on my life, I owe it all to being an entrepreneur. I took risks—many times. I succeeded—many times. I failed—not as often, but enough where I never forgot the lessons I learned.

Please allow my experiences and my enthusiasm for becoming an entrepreneur to be an encouragement to you as I come to the close of *Launching the Entrepreneur Ship*. One of my favorite inspirational quotes for entrepreneurs comes from British poet Alfred Lord Tennyson, who wrote, "Tis better to have loved and lost than never to have loved at all."

If you've been thinking about whether to go for it, I can't tell you whether you should or should not proceed with your business idea since I don't know the particulars. But I can encourage you to get in the game. I can remind you to ask people you respect what they think of your idea. I can prompt you to listen to what they have to say. And I can reiterate the importance of figuring out the next step and what you have to do to get there.

Only you can weigh the risks and decide whether to launch or not. Just as Mennonites, as a rule, don't gamble, neither should you as an entrepreneur. Just as a poker player doesn't bet his entire stash on the first hand of Texas Hold 'Em, you have to play smart too. Husband your resources. Play your cards when the odds seem in your favor. Invest your winnings into the next round and the round after that.

The old adage that it's two steps forward and one step back is so true when it comes to being an entrepreneur. There will be setbacks. There will be some hairy moments. There may be even some days when you wonder, *What the heck was I thinking?*

I also realize that not everyone is called to be a "business entrepreneur," but I encourage you wherever you are—in a non-profit or in academia—to embrace an entrepreneurial spirit and apply many of the principles in this book to the organizations you serve. The growth today of "social entrepreneurs" and B Corps is exciting to see and enables many who are passionate about making this a better world to build a sustainable organization.

My advice is to stay the course, whatever your passion, but don't get in a rut. Ask what you can do to build a better organization. Can you help turn things around? Do you need to find a better-value vendor? Do you need more inventory on hand to handle upswings in business? Can you develop a better social media strategy that ensures plenty of positive reviews on Yelp, Trip Advisor, or Angie's List?

Above all, think of others before yourself. Focus on the customer. Uphold the dignity of all people. Follow your passion. Be ethical in your dealings. Be true to yourself. Give back to your community and the world. And remember to persevere!

I've heard many successful entrepreneurs tell me, "Allon, you won't believe how close I was to packing it in." Sure, you'll sometimes feel like calling it quits or return to something safer, but something greater might be just around the corner.

So here are my final words to remember:

1. My *encouragement* to you is to act on your idea.

2. My *advice* to you is for you to do your homework by putting into writing your Vision Statement, Values Statement, Annual Plan, and Strategic Plan.

3. My *hope* for you is to operate from your values.

4. My *wish* for you is to make a successful launch and experience smoother-than-expected sailing.

5. My *prayer* for you is to become fulfilled as a values-centered entrepreneur.

No matter where you live in this crazy world, there is room for entrepreneurship. Follow your passion, find a way to share your talents, and launch your ship.

And know that I'm cheering you on.

ACKNOWLEDGMENTS

When you've known thousands of working associates, hundreds of friends from around the world, scores of church and community friends, and dozens of Board of Director associates, teachers, and students, where do you start with acknowledging their help and encouragement?

It's easy for me to begin with my wife, Doris, who's been my soulmate, my best friend, and the mother to our children and grandmother to our grandchildren. She has stood by me with unflagging support on almost every crazy entrepreneurial idea I've ever wanted to try. Thank you, Doris, for making my life meaningful, fun, and fulfilling through your love.

Next are my children, Rodney, Jeffrey and Debra, and the many ways they teach me the true joys of life as we enjoy being a family together.

As for others, I'm reluctant to call out specific names since starting and stopping is an almost impossible task. As I think back on my life, the mentorship of my father, Elvin, was instrumental in my development. He was supplemented by many good teachers and pastors in churches I attended over the years, for which I am eternally grateful.

In terms of business, I was blessed to have worked for two men of the highest integrity: Dale Weaver, the president of Victor F. Weaver, Inc., and Dale High, the president of High Industries, Inc. Both of these men successfully led mid-sized family businesses by a set of clear values, which helped them form a caring work culture. They were outstanding mentors to me, helping me realize the importance of values and culture in the pursuit of business.

I am so grateful for my longtime business associate and friend Carlton Miller and business partners such as Gerald Horst and Carl Harman, who were instrumental in their support as we worked together is numerous capacities over the years.

I've had many Board associates who were each dispensers of wisdom as we gave direction and guidance to corporations and not-for-profit firms. Leaders of non-profits such as Allan Sauder, president of MEDA, and Cary Summers, president of Museum of the Bible, were inspirations to me as I became involved in their outreaches to others.

When I moved into the academic arena for seven years, my professor colleagues taught me a great deal from their experiences. I was blessed to work for two great leaders in education: Dr. Shirley Showalter, president of Goshen College, and Dr. Beryl Brubaker, provost at Eastern Mennonite University. My work with LCC International University in Lithuania and President Dr. Marlene Wall has been especially inspiring.

My undertaking of *Launching the Entrepreneurial Ship* was consistently encouraged by my good friend Edgar Stoesz. Without his gentle but regular insistence that I put my entrepreneurial passion and story into a book, I may have been too busy doing other entrepreneurial things. Carol Hamilton, professor at James Madison University reviewed the manuscript through the eyes on one who teaches about entrepreneurship, and Stephanie Zayhowski read through the eyes of a Millennial. Their suggestions were extremely helpful. And finally, a great big thank you to my co-author, Mike Yorkey, who was a joy to work with as he helped me shape and improve my thoughts. And thanks to Keely Boeving of WordServe Literary for her editing and layout help.

My debt is broad for the many hundreds of you—my friends, my business associates, and my students—who have shaped my worldview and helped me to better appreciate the ways that each one of us can contribute to making this a better world.

ABOUT THE AUTHORS

Allon Lefever, the author of *Launching the Entrepreneur Ship*, is president of Lefever Associates, a consulting firm. He currently performs executive and entrepreneurship coaching with a specialty in mergers and acquisition, strategic planning, and board development work. He is also president of A Better Hospitality Company, an owner and operator of hotels.

After graduating magna cum laude from Millersville State College and earning a Master's in Economics from Penn State University, he started his corporate career in 1980 with Victor F. Weaver, Inc. Within seven years of joining the company, he assumed overall responsibility for the operations division. When Weaver was sold to Holly Farms, he resigned and joined High Industries, where he served as senior manager for a number of years and helped revenue grow from $200 million to $400 million.

While he was at High Industries, his son, Rod, suggested that they start one of the first Internet Service Providers (ISP) in southeast Pennsylvania in 1993. Getting in on the ground floor in the Internet world eventually led to merging with other regional ISPs that were eventually purchased by EarthLink in 2001.

After leaving the tech industry in his mid-fifties, Allon moved into education and became the executive director of the Goshen Family Business Program at Goshen University in Goshen, Indianan as well as an associate professor in the Business department. After two years in Goshen, he was hired by Eastern Mennonite University in Harrisonburg, Virginia, to direct the school's Master of Business Administration program.

After leaving the education field in 2008, Allon has remained active in a variety of entrepreneurial efforts as well as running a successful consulting business.

He has been married to Doris for more than fifty years, and they are the parents of three adult children—Rod, Jeff, and Debra—and ten wonderful grandchildren. They continue to make their hometown of Lancaster, Pennsylvania.

His website is www.LaunchingtheEntrepreneurShip.com.

Mike Yorkey is the author or co-author of one hundred books with more than 2 million copies in print. He has collaborated with Tampa Bay Rays' Ben Zobrist and his wife, Julianna, a Christian music artist, in *Double Play*; Cleveland Browns quarterback Colt McCoy and his father, Brad, in *Growing Up Colt*; San Francisco Giants pitcher Dave Dravecky in *Called Up*; San Diego Chargers placekicker Rolf Benirschke in *Alive & Kicking*; tennis star Michael Chang in *Holding Serve*; and paralyzed Rutgers' defensive tackle Eric LeGrand in *Believe: My Faith and the Tackle That Changed My Life*. Mike is also the co-author of the internationally bestselling *Every Man's Battle* series with Steve Arterburn and Fred Stoeker. He has written several fiction books, including *The Swiss Courier* and *Chasing Mona Lisa*.

He and his wife, Nicole, are the parents of two adult children and make their home in Encinitas, California.

Mike's website is www.mikeyorkey.com.

INVITE ALLON LEFEVER TO SPEAK

Allon Lefever is a dynamic speaker with a passion to inspire the next generation of entrepreneurs. He has spoken all over the world about entrepreneurship and how you can start your own business, and he has a passion to make a positive contribution to the development of the next generation of business and organization leaders.

If you, your community group, college or university, or high school would be interested in having Allon speak, please contact him at (540) 421-6888 or by email at allon.lefever@emu.edu or at www.LaunchingtheEntrepreneurShip.com.

For bulk purchases of *Launching the Entrepreneur Ship,* please contact Allon Lefever.